C. D. Harper is a retired Professor of Theatre Arts and Dance at California State University, Los Angeles, where he served as Chair of the Department of Theatre Arts, Founding Executive Director of the Harriet and Charles Luckman Fine Arts Complex, Founder of the Luckman Jazz Orchestra. He also served as Executive Assistant to the President of the University. He received an undergraduate degree from the University of Illinois, and a Master and Ph.D. from St. Louis University. Dr. Harper has published two novels: Covenant and Face the Unknown. He resides in Gleneden Beach, Oregon.

WITHOUT REDEMPTION

C.D. Harper

Without Redemption
Copyright © 2021 by C.D. Harper. All rights reserved.

No part of this publication may be reproduced, stored in a retrieval system or transmitted in any way by any means, electronic, mechanical, photocopy, recording or otherwise without the prior permission of the author except as provided by USA copyright law.

This novel is a work of fiction. Names, descriptions, entities, and incidents included in the story are products of the author's imagination. Any resemblance to actual persons, events, and entities is entirely coincidental.

The opinions expressed by the author are not necessarily those of URLink Print and Media.

1603 Capitol Ave., Suite 310 Cheyenne, Wyoming USA 82001
1-888-980-6523 | admin@urlinkpublishing.com

URLink Print and Media is committed to excellence in the publishing industry.

Book design copyright © 2021 by URLink Print and Media. All rights reserved.

Published in the United States of America

Library of Congress Control Number: 2021909016
ISBN 978-1-64753-789-0 (Paperback)
ISBN 978-1-64753-790-6 (Digital)

21.04.21

For Linda Kostalik, my wife.

Thanks to Liz Locke, Shelby Locke and Tamara Jones.

Contents

The Dark Place 11

Only When He Was With Them 26

Walter 81

Walter's Line 100

Without Redemption 116

The Dark Place

Joseph stood there, not paralyzed but realizing for the first time his loneliness and his limitations, wishing he had accepted Captain Ben's offer and said 'yes' to God who then would become his provider and protector, his navigator and his master. At least then he would be able to pray for help and expect His hand of mercy to reach down and lead and protect him. Instead he chose to face the unknown alone.

Captain Ben had tried to convince him that his God was the creator of all tomorrows and had the answer to whatever tomorrow would bring. Joseph, however, had decided during the fiery destruction of the Settlement, his home, to challenge the unknown, but he didn't realize its magnitude or what it really required or meant.

Joseph knew he had arrived at a point of desperation. Even if he had accepted Captain Ben's God, what would that have meant? Was it the end of slavery and a better life? What would that be to him? He wasn't a slave and had never been a slave. Yet, he was running, looking, hoping for that safe place to be, just like all the slaves he had ever met who stopped at the Settlement to shed their all-consuming slave armor and become ex-slaves.

Everything he knew and remembered existed because of slavery, even for him, the never-been-a-slave. Slavery, he was learning, determined everything, and everything determined slavery, North and South. It was manifested in the do's and don'ts of facial features; in words spoken, stories told and imagined; and in the laws written and ignored, customs formulated and realized, and in feelings expressed and hidden; in an American creed written but not followed. And always, in the color of one's skin.

He looked around for a tree, not any tree, but that special tree that miraculously had always been there when he needed it. But not this time. There was no tree, no branches reaching and stretching; there were only bushes, weeds, sticky shrubbery, tall grass, and a path that led into the unknown.

Time had lost much of its meaning for Joseph. He knew there was daylight when he would hide and close his eyes and rest. And when sleep came, those horrors of the past filled his sleep with familiar images: the fire that consumed his community of free men and women and slaves and exslaves, his attempt to escape the screams for help, the smell of burning human flesh, and finally those burred images of white men looking down on him, the blackout and the ship's crew who determined he was a slave and insisted he act like one.

Then, night would slowly and quietly come with its own hidden paths and secrets, allowing him to quietly move through its darkness in search of that special place to be.

Joseph heard a rustling sound, like something was moving through the brush and headed his way. It was a big and intrusive sound, like it was supposed to scare whatever was in its path. At first, he thought it was Thomas, but he was too thin and slight of spirit to create such a huge uproar. While Thomas may have been taught to kill slave mongers, he didn't seem to have the will to be otherwise aggressive. He was, after all, the house butler, or house nigger, in the home of a wealthy Rhode Islander. Joseph had concluded that Thomas had no heart for pursuing the unknown. He was content to struggle with the known way of life based on slavery.

"Thomas? Thomas, is that you?" Joseph called out to him loudly, knowing there would be no answer. But he refused to give up. There was then a softer call. "Thomas?" And his final effort was really for himself. "Are you there, Thomas?" It was a murmur, inaudible. How foolish, he thought, even shameful. Why would Thomas have followed him? Surely, he had his own life to pursue, his own struggles.

In the next moment, powerful images of Joseph's past flashed across his mind. He resisted, but they were all he had, all he knew. There could never be flashes of tomorrow, the unknown, because tomorrow was indeed tomorrow. Maybe Thomas knew this better than he did.

Maybe this was what Thomas saw in him, that refusal to except and struggle with the known and the fear of the unknown. Maybe Thomas was the rustling sound he'd heard earlier. Perhaps he had been following him, spying on him, seeing, and sensing his fear.

Joseph felt defenseless and angry with himself for submitting to ordinary human frailty. If he were really planning on the pursuit of the unknown by himself, he discovered he needed to be better prepared.

When he heard that sound again, his instincts took over and he ran up a steep path. This time, he didn't look back. He just ran as fast as he could up that steep hill to a plateau where he had to stop to catch his breath.

When he looked around, he discovered an area that looked like the dark place Thomas had described. It wasn't a large area, but it was distinctly different from everything around it. The surrounding flora stopped at its edges, setting it off from everything in sight. Joseph remembered that Thomas had never seen this special place. Mr. Ricardo had described it to him, which made Joseph wonder how much Thomas had learned on his own. Joseph had already become suspicious and had ignored him, never thinking he would ever encounter such a place, but there it was.

In a way, Joseph thought it was a unique thing of beauty, looking down at it from the plateau. There was a strange sameness of trees that he had never seen before. All of them were the same height with branches full of leaves, rendering the area underneath sunless and dark. It looked like it had been deliberately planned for that particular place for some particular reason.

He could see how a person could unintentionally walk right into it. Looking at it from the plateau, it looked harmless, but Thomas told a different story. And he had somehow been guided, perhaps with Thomas's phantom assistance, around its southern edge and up the hill where he had stopped to get his breath.

He concluded that he had overcome his first challenge, albeit with Thomas's help. He started to walk slowly away from the dark place. He felt the adrenaline rushing through his body, and it felt good. He was smiling. In the midst of all the uncertainty around him, he had somehow been successful. It was like he could hear every distinct sound in nature, feel every slight breeze that swept through each nook and cranny, and smell every scent that filled the air. He was alive and his eyes were bright and shiny.

At the end of the plateau, there was a road above it going west. But it was daylight, and Joseph needed to find a place to rest in preparation for his night's travels. He was excited but cautiously optimistic. There was a path, a way of going, that ran through the shrubbery not far from the road, which both intrigued and frightened him. But it also shepherded in the possibility of a better day. And every time he thought about that day, he gathered more strength. It could be the day he would find that special place, but then again, it may not be.

He stopped, not because he heard the rustling sound again, but because the sound of panting dogs was getting closer. His first thought was to run, but the dogs ran past him directly into the dark place before he could take a step. It was startling. It happened so quickly he had no time to think or react. Whatever scent they were on, it wasn't his.

The two colored men running behind the dogs saw him but kept running, following the dogs. The older of the two men was dressed in a seersucker suit; it was old and winkled, but a suit nonetheless. And he wore a dingy shirt and tie. On his head was a hat, which he had pulled down over his ears to keep it from blowing away, and over his shoulder was a bag that seemed to contain a book. The other younger man was muscular but rather thin and wore bib overalls without a shirt. They stopped at the edge of the dark place.

The one in the suit turned around and looked as if he were waiting for someone. There was a slight smile on his face. Joseph didn't know what to think, so he concluded they were hunting coons, rabbits, or possums. Then, he saw the three white men following, one on horseback.

"What's wrong with them dogs? Why they ain't barking no more?" one of the three white men spoke, but Joseph couldn't tell which one. He was sure however, it wasn't the one on the horse.

"'Cause they trained to hunt niggers quietly. They be up on niggers before they know it, so get ready." He was the different-looking one with red hair and clean clothes, riding a high-spirited brown horse that wouldn't be still.

When Joseph was a little boy, the African, back at the Settlement, he was one of its leaders, had told a story about the first white man he'd ever seen with red hair. He said it had almost scared him to death. He had never seen red hair before. And as Joseph thought about it, this was his first time, but it didn't scare him. It just looked very strange to see a person with red hair. To be born like that must have been some kind of trick or curse.

"Then, how we supposed to know where they at and stuff? It dark in there." The colored man at the edge of the dark place looked back at them for an answer.

"Don't matter. You get your black ass in there and find 'em. Go on; get in there," the redhead said. The other white men laughed.

"That nigger scared," one of the white men said. He was laughing and jumping around and grinning in a very weird way. He looked like he was related to the other lanky white man, although he was fat with a stomach that looked uncomfortably big. And he didn't seem to be able to stand still. It was like he couldn't stop his arms or legs or head from moving in a jerky way.

The white man on the horse was obviously in charge. Although it was clear that they had been on the road for a while, he looked the neatest with a little dust here and there, and he wore a hat that looked new. And from the saddle of his prancing horse, he looked down on the others and kept his distance from them.

"You suppose to follow 'em. Damn, y'all can't do nothing right, can you? They cornered. We got 'em. See? No dog barking. Why y'all stop now? Go get 'em," the lanky one shouted at the colored men, who appeared to be apprehensive about going farther but proceeded and quickly disappeared.

The two white men who looked somewhat like brothers had stopped at the edge of the road and were stretching and pointing and trying to look into the dark place. They couldn't have been more than a couple of hundred yards or so from Joseph. But they were so absorbed by the dark place and how quickly those colored boys had disappeared that they never looked his way.

"I told you what kind of dogs they was. Good dogs, I told you. And those niggers is good too. They been working together for a long time. If you want my dogs, you get my niggers. They know what to do. So, don't start looking at me like they ain't what I represented them to be. Get on in there and get 'em! The dogs done their part; now you do yours. Hell, the niggers done more than you. Get on in there." The redhead remained on his horse up on the road, looking down into the dark place and watching the brothers. He had one hand on the reins and the other on his pistol.

"I don't think . . . you know what? I'm willing to bet they ain't even in there no more. Them boys don't know what they doing, or they would have waited for them to come out. That nigger in that suit? He don't know nothing." The lanky one in the bib overalls and tattered shirt had a shiny new looking shotgun. And he held it out for the redhead to see. "Maybe I should shoot in there a couple times. See what happens."

"And kill my dogs and niggers? I'd have to shoot you then." The redhead was laughing, but it was clear he was serious.

"They ain't nothing but niggers. Hell, you can get more of them anytime," the shaky one spoke, with an equal amount of seriousness.

"The one in the suit? He's a preacher man. He carries his Bible in that little sack around his neck. He ain't no ordinary nigger." The redhead seemed to be proud of his nigger.

"Bet that nigger can't even read. Tell you something else. If he can read . . . that ain't good. 'Cause then, he can read anything, the Bible, them pamphlets, anything, just like some of us. That ain't good, I tell you. Then them niggers think that know as much as you or me or my brother here. Killing him might be the best thing to do." The shaky one moved so much his word seemed to vibrate in the air.

"Hush up! We got stuff to do here. You don't know what you talking about anyway." The lanky one turned his attention back to the dark place.

"You never read the Bible. Shit, you can't read nothing. When Mama was learning me to read, you was out running around like a crazy person. See, she told you. But you didn't have time. All you knew to do was chase them gals. Mama told you one day you gonna need her learning."

"Hush, Paul. That's all you know how to do is talk and shake. Just hush up." The lanky one took a step down the hill closer to the dark place.

"I ain't hushing up nothing. Mama told you, you can't tell me what to do. I ain't shaking much. I'm all right." Paul's movements, even walking, raising his arms and everything about him, seemed deliberate and slow. It was like he had to think before moving. He even turned his head slowly, this way and that way, like he had to search to find the right button to activate in order to move.

"That reading shit ain't got nothing to do with us catching and selling niggers, and we better do it while we can. Niggers gonna be gone soon just like them Indians.

Where, I don't know. Then, what we gonna do? Huh?" the lanky one spoke up quickly, as if to dismiss what his brother, Paul, was saying.

"Hey, y'all hush up and get on in there! I ain't got all day," the red head spoke, as he worked to control his horse.

"They could be hiding in there, waiting, them and their sympathizers. Look how dark it is in there. Hell, you won't be able to see them anyway. We better do something quick. What you think, Paul?" It was difficult to know if that was a serious question or not, because he had already moved closer.

The redhead's horse started acting nervous, moving around, and he had to restrain it again. "See, my horse is ready to go. He got a young mare back there in the barn waiting for him," he chuckled.

"Know what?" The brothers started talking to each other like the man on the horse wasn't there. All the redhead did was look from one to the other.

Joseph, meanwhile, remained motionless in fear of being detected. The three men were absorbed in their own drama, and Joseph didn't want to become part of it.

"They got help, you know, them abolition folks. Could be a whole lot of them in there. Most of them white too. 'Course, we would see them, the white ones. I . . . I don't see any from here. They must be back in there somewhere. You know, put the niggers out front first."

"That's the way they do, ain't it? That's what mama said." Paul, the shaky one, nodded his head to confirm the true of what he had just said.

"Mama ain't known nothing about no abolition folks. Hey, in there! What you niggers doing, huh? What done happened to them dogs?" If he had taken another step or two, he would have been inside the dark place. He still strained to see into the dark woods.

Paul was doing the same thing, but he was standing farther up the side of that little hill, trying desperately to maintain his balance and control his shaking.

Joseph thought about running but realized he didn't know where to run, and the redhead on that horse didn't give him much chance of succeeding.

"That nigger preacher man . . . if he got that Bible, we all right. It's our Bible, ain't it? We wrote it, didn't we? So don't worry. The good Lord will take care of everything," the lanky one spoke, and the brother and he looked at each other for confirmation.

"Hell, how you know that?" The redhead, who hadn't spoken for a while, shook his head. "My dogs know what to do. 'Cause you don't hear them don't mean nothing."

"How you know so much? You know more than God? That nigger preacher man knows what to do. All we got to do is wait a minute or two."

"Then, what?" the redhead spoke quickly.

"You just sit there on that horse and hush up. Don't seem like you know much, if you ask me." The lanky one walked back to the horse. He held up his new-looking shotgun, all shiny, to his chest like he might have to use it.

"Better not get too close. She doesn't take to strangers. Back away, back away! She gets fussy sometimes." The redhead seemed to urge his horse toward the lanky one.

The brothers looked at each other, and the redhead laughed.

"What you laughing at?" the lanky one asked. "You better not be laughing at my brother. He can't help it. The Lord made him that way for a reason."

"I wasn't laughing at your brother. I was laughing at you. Now get your lazy ass in there and run them niggers out here. Get! Let's get our minds on what we out here for, and that's to get Mr. Levine's niggers back. If there are others, you can have 'em. He just wants what's his."

"Heck, we don't even know if they came this way. They could be anywhere, even back in New York," the lanky one said.

"My dogs got their scent. They in there. Go get 'em." They didn't hear the dogs anymore or anything else. That fact seemed to unsettle them, along with not being able to see into the woods. The brothers never looked at the redhead and his horse again. They were absorbed with the prospect of having to follow the dogs into the dark place.

The lanky twin then spoke quietly, almost to himself, as he walked back to the edge of the dark place. "Wonder what done happen to them dogs? That must be a sign of something. I don't know what, but something."

Joseph noticed the other brother's hand shook more when he would try to reach for his brother

"Damn, it done got quiet, ain't it?" The lanky one looked into the darkness nervously. "What y'all boys got in there?" He had moved closer, stepping in front of his brother with his shotgun in the ready position and straining to see into the darkness. He moved even closer to the first trees of the dark place, a bit beyond his brother's shaking reach.

"You in there, y'all see anything? Ain't got a lot of time to be fooling around, you know." His shaking affected his speech, making it less clear, almost like a loud mumble. He continued to reach for his twin's arm with his shaking hand, moving forward just a bit but not close enough to touch him.

Then, there was an excruciatingly long squeal and howl from the dogs.

"Oh, shit. Oh, shit. Them niggers done killed the dogs. Lord, have mercy. What we gonna do now?" This was almost clearly spoken. "If they think they can just up and kill our dogs, what they think next?" He was jumping up and down, and his brother looked back at him.

"Done had enough. Y'all gonna get it now. We still running things around here and always will. Y'all done upset my brother, and I ain't liking that one bit. You stay right there and stop that damn shaking." He took two steps into the woods, looking back like he expected the redheaded man to follow. "Y'all come on now. You niggers hear me? I can smell niggers a mile away, so I know you in here. Here I come. You stay put, Paul. Seems like I'm always saving your shaking ass." The lanky one proceeded farther into the dark place.

"Hey, wait a minute. You can't leave me. Mama told you about leaving me. Don't you leave me out here by myself! I can't go in there. I don't like the dark. We don't have to. Do we?" He looked at the redhead for an answer.

"I don't know what you're saying," the redhead spoke rather calmly.

"My brother said we still in charge." He was trying to slow down his speech so the redhead could understand him, but he was too excited.

"Y'all coming?" The lanky one had gone so far into the dark place they couldn't see him.

"You come on out of there. Mama told you. I don't like being by myself. Best come back here with me. Come on. You hear me?" His speech became louder and unclear.

Just then, a voice came from the woods.

"I am the way, the truth, and the life. No man cometh unto the Father but through me." There was silence.

"What? What was that? Who said that? What's he talking about?" Paul seemed to crumble on the hillside.

The redhead moved his horse around nervously, but he offered no response.

The silence continued.

"That ain't nothing but that nigger preacher trying to scare us, ain't it? That ain't even what the Bible says, is it? Come on out of there. You . . . you know what Mama said."

"Don't look like you two will get anything done here. Best be heading back toward home. Don't ask me about no pay, 'cause you ain't getting none. Hell, my dogs and niggers worth more than you and your brother." The redhead moved his horse to the other side of the road.

Joseph was sure he saw him, but he turned his back.

"Don't you come back without Mr. Levine's niggers," the redhead said. "You hear me?"

"We can't leave him in there by himself." Paul tried to back up, shaking and stumbling. "What if they done circled around behind him with a bunch of mean-looking niggers and got him cornered like he some animal or something? Then what? I don't know what to do." He was becoming so shaky, Joseph was sure if he were a few feet closer he would hear them.

There was silence as the redhead moved farther away, urging his horse into a trot and never looking back.

"What we gonna do? They may be behind us and in front of us. Where we go? Hey, what we gonna do?" Paul watched the redhead as his horse continued farther and farther down the road.

"Hold on there. Don't leave me. I can't be by myself. Mama said I couldn't." He stood there looking into the woods where his brother had gone, and for the redhead, who had turned onto the field, the same one they had come out of, and then, disappeared.

There was a thudding sound and a surprised scream for help. Then, there was silence. Absolute silence, no birds, no crickets, or other critters, nothing.

"Where y'all at? I can't see nothing." Paul was standing at the edge of the woods, straining to see inside and backing up at the same time. Clearly, he wanted to go after his brother, but fear overcame him, and his body seemed to collapse. He would try to stand again but each time he would collapse.

Joseph watched Paul try to climb the hill up to the road, but he couldn't. He tried time and time again, struggling as he crawled forward as best he could with his mouth open and saliva running down his chin. Tears ran down his cheeks, and his arms reached for something or someone to help him, but no one was there. Then he saw Joseph.

Joseph, realizing the shaky one had seen him, took off running. The shaky one's response was a typical one. He reached for his pistol. His jerky hand movements and shaky body caused him to shoot himself in the leg as he attempted to pull out his pistol, and he screamed.

"Help me, nigga! Come back here! Help me! Don't leave me, nigga. Nigga . . . "

Joseph didn't look back. He kept running until he was exhausted. His knees shook and hurt, and the muscles in his legs trembled. He wanted to run more but couldn't; he had run far enough. At least, he couldn't hear that word anymore.

Maybe it was that word that had pushed him farther and harder. That one word symbolized everything he was trying to get away from—the artificial world of the Settlement and the thoughts and vivid images of the fire and Captain Ben's Christian world and the many stories

and tales of the slaves and ex-slaves and masters and overseers, everything.
He was out of breath. He thought about turning and looking back, but he didn't. He knew what the past was and what it wasn't. The chronicle of those images was etched across his mind and reappeared at will. At first, he tried to walk slowly, hoping to catch his breath. But he found himself walking faster and faster until he was trotting and looking around.

Then, he found himself running and looking around. He didn't know why, but that's what he did. That was his comfort zone, the run from some known place to some unknown place.

He remembered leaning on that perfect tree and thinking, knowing he could climb as high as he wanted and find that branch, that perfect branch that reached and stretched outward and upward. Each year, it reached farther and stretched farther. It was like his running here and there, pausing, running again, reaching, and stretching!

(Ain't gonna let nobody turn me around.)

Only When He Was With Them

There was a pretty good reason Christopher was sitting on that tree stump that day, right by the doorway to that shack, which wasn't really a shack. It had the makings of a real fine dwelling, better than any of the shacks on Slaves' Road. Christopher was a master craftsman, a carpenter of extraordinary skill. Miss Madie Marie Princeton, Dexter Princeton's wife, had insisted he learn a good trade because she was certain slavery wasn't going to last much longer. And she told him so, along with anybody else who would listen.

And Christopher knew she was right, not because she said it and she was a white lady, but because the grapevine had that information days ago. He knew something she didn't know. The Blue Coats were coming their way, and many of them were ex-slaves. He learned that through the grapevine, and more than that, when he put his ear to the ground, he could hear them coming, at least that's what he said.

In addition to carpentry, she had insisted he learn everything he could about whatever there was to learn. So, he learned to read and write and do his numbers and to think like Mr. Dexter and her. This had served him well, but only when he was with them. And there were other things she allowed him to learn about her that were absolutely unacceptable in the antebellum culture of the South.

Most folks wanted to blame Madie Marie for Mr. Dexter's peculiar ways, because she was bred and educated in the North. But people who knew his family history weren't surprised at all. It was Shelton Princeton, the first Princeton to arrive in this British American colony in the early 1700s from Sheffield, England, who had been given the land to cultivate. Back then slaves and indentured servants, that's what some of them were called and really treated like slaves, were brought from a variety of places throughout the world to work the land.

Mr. Princeton, he made a point of telling everybody, who would listen, his interest in slavery and indentured servants was all very temporary and just a means to get started in the potentially prolific gold mining business.

The Princeton family was in the metal business, had business tentacles throughout the British Empire, especially African and India, and was quite wealthy. So the fact that Shelton was in the British American Colony searching for gold to further the family's enterprise was expected and accepted as part of the purpose of the English Empire and the Princeton family business, which some folk thought was really exploitation.

The family was very serious, as were many other wealthy British families, about their responsibility to Christianize, capitalize, and foster their notion of civilization throughout the world. That, after all, was what the colonies were for.

This venture in the new world was to give Shelton breathing space so he could establish his own wealth and family line, while enhancing his family's position and status throughout the Empire, making his family and England proud.

When Shelton was a boy, his father, Adam, had warned him about his Uncle Herman, who had left for a place in Africa called the Congo in search of his fortune but had not been seen or heard from since. He was, among the Shelton boys, the handsome one with muscles and a fine-looking black mustache. He was also the example Shelton was not to follow, at least, that was the instruction his father had given him.

Shelton assured them that he would not fail and that the Princeton name would not be associated with slavery for very long. His gold and silver prospecting prospects were extremely good. And that was what the family was really interested in. His success, however, was directly related to the hard work of mining, and that would be done by slaves or indentured labor.

So, when Dexter's time came to manage the Princeton Manor, it came as no surprise to his family that he selected a refined, educated Northerner to marry. But first she had to travel to Sheffield for the Princeton family's approval, which was greatly enhanced by her view that slavery was indeed a temporary endeavor. And she quickly won their approval, of course.

They were married in Sheffield and spent their first night together aboard the good ship, the Princeton Endeavor, which was owned by the Princeton family. In its day it was a prominent and profitable freighter, transporting cargo of rum, food, other commodities and several Africans, but was no longer directly in the slave trade business. The ship had been converted to a cargo vessel, which ran the same route the slave ships did and carried goods from slave labor. The cargo actually could not have been produced without slavery.

Slavery, as practiced by the New World, was central to the economy of the British Empire, a fact the Princeton family chose to ignore. What they did celebrate was the new English law prohibiting slave ships from anchoring in its waters. Thus, Princeton Endeavor became a cargo ship, and England became quite proud of itself.

The wedding night had proven to be a bit bumpy. Dexter didn't seem to be very adept at exploring wedding night treats. He knew where to go but not what to do once he got there. It was his first time with a white lady, and it clearly had to be more than getting in and getting out.

She had far more experience. There were many bouts with a cousin, who was a bit older and had shown her how to enjoy the moment. Her expectations were well established. Dexter had much to learn, but she told herself she would pretend to be just as naive.

After the ship docked in New Orleans, they were ushered onto a paddle steamer for the trip up the Mississippi, which was done with maximum fanfare and comfort for Dexter and his new bride, who was getting all the attention a Princeton bride should expect, except she didn't seem too comfortable or impressed, especially given that all the work was done by slaves. Dexter whispered something in her ear, and she seemed to relax until the canoe, which was to take them to the pier for the train ride to Four Point City and the Princeton Manor.

They both appeared to be quite happy. She was confident she would bring him around to more satisfying bedtime experiences. But he wasn't so confident. She was a bit disappointed, however, to discover an abundance of slaves working in the fields and everywhere. She confessed to him how surprised she was that the Princeton family not only was in the gold business but also had interest in cotton and anything else that would grow, including timber, especially since the family had convinced her that they, like her family, were longtime Christians and supported a future without slavery. She was young, of course, and had not discovered the contradictions necessary and perhaps engrained in the pursuit of wealth and empire.

Somewhere between Shelton and Dexter, some American Princeton family members had discovered that slavery was just as profitable as the mining for gold, if not more, and certainly less unpredictable.

While the Princeton family remained committed Christians, they had stopped giving and going to church years ago. They had hoped to eliminate Christianity as an obvious concern in their pursuit of wealth and influence.

The talk about slavery being temporary, especially on the mainland, remained a viable conversation in reference to the Princeton dynasty. They were known to be practical in their pursuit of wealth, which often required compromises on many fronts.

While their duplicity was often a topic of discussion and fascination, they did indeed profit and gather enormous personal benefit from slavery. What they did differently, however, was how they treated their people. And Christopher was the most obvious benefactor of that treatment. It was well known that Christopher was not the head nigger, but more like the son Mr. Dexter and Madie Marie didn't have.

As a matter of fact, there was no head nigger at Princeton Manor. That word, nigger, was not used there. Slaves were called Dexter's people. And their people gave of their labor out of love and appreciation and admiration for the Princeton family and their way of life. Their people wanted them to be happy and prosperous, even at the expense of their own possibilities.

Christopher, however, spent most of his time in the house, not as a servant but as someone who simply lived there as part of the family. But there was more to Christopher. He seemed to understand that slavery actually protected him. But as the Blue Coats marched toward Princeton Manor, that protection was about to be stripped away, and Madie Marie's prediction that slavery would end would be realized. Christopher would have to learn to live and struggle like a freed man. And he seemed to know that time was near, not that he understood what that would mean or what his responsibilities would be.

But before slavery ended and the soldiers' arrival, he found himself in the middle of Madie Marie and Mr. Dexter's relationship. Lillie Lee was the woman Mr. Dexter wanted him to mate with. He didn't object since she was indeed desirable and the pick of the litter. But she wasn't his choice. She was Mr. Dexter's choice.

Christopher was given, by Mr. Dexter, the permission, the lumber, and the time to build a shack for Lillie Lee and himself, because he was a firm believer in good breeding. Although marriage was impossible among their people at the Manor, Mr. Dexter did attempt to keep his people together as families when possible. And Mr. Dexter would have been delighted and happy keeping Christopher and Lillie Lee together. That, in his mind, was the coming together of good stock, not to mention getting Christopher out of his house and away from Madie Marie.

But Christopher was never able to finish the project because Miss Madie Marie found out about it and made him stop the building and the mating, at least, those were her intentions and Christopher's instructions.

From that day on, she made sure Christopher slept in the house in the little room upstairs just off her and Mr. Dexter's bedroom. It was a small room but large enough for him to have a bed and for her to visit periodically. Consequently, in her mind, there was no need for him to have a personal shack, fancy or otherwise, or a relationship with Lillie Lee. So the shack was never finished.

Miss Madie Marie was quite pleased and delighted when Mr. Dexter told her about Christopher's coffin-making skills. It could become a full-time pursuit, keeping him busy and away from Lillie Lee's shack. Then, there was the future when slavery would be over; Christopher would have a trade, a means of supporting himself.

"Did Chris and some of our people cut that big old tree down? The one you said didn't look right?" She was smiling, happy to have Chris's attention back. Of course, she already knew about the tree because Chris had told her and sometimes he would be covered with sawdust.

"Yep, we had to cut it down," Mr. Dexter was smiling.

"Who's going to finish that gal Lillie Lee's shack?"

"Oh, I don't know. We'll get around to it one day. Hell, we got so much timber from that tree, Christopher will be making coffins for a long, long time, fancy ones too."

They were both happy and had big smiles on their faces.

"Well, why don't you go into the timber business full time, Dexter? Then, you could stop all this slavery business. Probably make your family happy."

"Maybe, but what would my people do? They love working for us. They are so happy. My family is happy too. Money makes them happy. Having my people working in the fields is the best moneymaker right now. Plus, I'm not sure we'll ever have a tree like that again. Takes years to grow like that. That tree was hundred years old or more, maybe. It was probably a little thing when the first Princeton got here."

It had been the biggest and tallest and the most distinct tree in the entire area, looking regal and seen from miles and miles away. But, it consumed too much space. Nothing would grow around or underneath it. It seemed to consume all that energy for itself.

One of his really old people told him the tree was dying and needed to come down to prevent it from suffering. Then, he assured Mr. Dexter that God would not be angry with him.

Mr. Dexter didn't know what to do. The tree was certainly different, like it wasn't supposed to be there, yet it was. And as far as Mr. Dexter knew, there wasn't a similar tree growing anywhere in the area.

"No hangings from that tree," he used to say to himself. "Not on Princeton land. Damn good tree. Maybe that's why it's so tall and used to look so regal. Time changes everything, the good and the bad."

And below ground, Mr. Dexter told Christopher he couldn't imagine what its root structure was like, how deep it ran and how far it reached, and he wasn't sure if they could ever shovel deep enough or far enough to dig it out.

Cutting the tree down had been more of a production than Mr. Dexter or Christopher had anticipated. It took weeks of climbing and sawing just to get down to the massive trunk, and then, more weeks to get the timber in usable shape. Christopher's carpentry shop was full. Overrun, surrounded with wood from that massive tree. But it was more than just an abundance of lumber. For him, it provided the wood for the porch he built for Madie Marie and Mr. Dexter and the shack he was going to build for Lillie Lee and himself.

When the weather was nice, Miss Madie Marie and Mr. Dexter would sit on that porch for their morning coffee or afternoon glass of lemonade. And Christopher would sit on the steps, right below them, although Madie Marie always had a chair available for him.

Sometimes he would have a glass of lemonade, but never coffee. And the maid who served them often smiled at Christopher, even that slight gesture of bowing in his direction went unnoticed by Madie Marie and Mr. Dexter. But Christopher noticed, and it made him uncomfortable. He was not one of them, wanting her to bow to him. He was special, yes, and required special attention, true.

They'd sit there, the three of them, and talk back and forth about the news in the pamphlets and newspapersitl and magazines and political letters and the latest rumors, mostly about the end of slavery and how that would affect the other slave owners, not Mr. Dexter, but always the other owners.

It was like he wasn't a slave owner. Of course, he never bought a slave. His family's tradition emphasized breeding, sometimes with other owners, but more often than not among his own people. Money was never involved, no selling or buying of slaves for Mr. Dexter.

Because Christopher could read, Miss Madie Marie made sure he read the same newspapers and pamphlets they did. Some mornings they would sit and read and talk.

"Did you read this, Dexter? Chris? It's one of those things from that South Carolina newspaper talking about how runaway slaves are being killed and saying slavery will never end. Doesn't that bother you, Chris? And all this talk about the Union Army having colored soldiers now, with rifles and all?" She paused and looked at Christopher for a long moment. "Would you like to join up, Chris?"

"Now, Madie Marie, this doesn't have anything to do with Christopher, or us for that matter. He's . . . all my people are doing just fine."

"Slavery is wrong, Dexter, just wrong. And it's going to end. This . . . what's happening now . . . just might be the start."

"Maybe! I just don't know if they're ready for it. That's the only thing."

"Are you ready for it?" She looked directly at Dexter.

"Don't be looking at me like that. You know I'm not like the others."

"I know, I know! We do better, don't we? You're a good man, Dexter."

It was quiet for a moment. Then, Christopher looked up to them and said, "It's going to be all right. Slavery will be over soon." He smiled and returned to reading and sipping his lemonade. He didn't know how he would have answered Madie Marie's question. He hadn't really thought about joining up. If he had, he probably would have said so.

"Then what, Chris? What? After slavery, I mean." She was now sitting on the edge of her chair, looking directly at Chris.

"They would have to find their own place. Can't stay here. Can you imagine? What a mess that would be," Mr. Dexter interceded and spoke with assurance and confidence.

"One thing at a time, I guess." Christopher was obviously disturbed. "Slavery ending first, then we'll see."

"Maybe we're moving too fast. Best slow down." Mr. Dexter nodded his head, adding more significance to what he had just said.

"They aren't worried about that. No such thing as too fast!" Christopher responded quickly.

"They?" Mr. Dexter looked puzzled.

"He's not one of them, Dexter," Madie Marie looked agitated.

"Yeah, I know. He's not one of us either. No matter what we said or do . . . or try. He's different from us."

"Am I? A cat can't have a baby by a dog, can it?" Christopher smiled. "Don't worry slavery is ending. That's what you want, right?"

Christopher's confidence did cause them, especially Mr. Dexter, some discomfort. They, Mr. Dexter and Madie Marie, didn't have access to the Underground Railroad. All they had were the newspapers and pamphlets. Sometimes, the information could be weeks old.

Mr. Dexter thought their reputation and history for humane treatment was sufficient for his people. It wasn't.

Christopher knew this. They thought they knew too, but they didn't.

It was admirable to have the idea and even the belief that slavery would end. But when the idea and belief were about to become a reality, then a very different attitude, vision, and behavior emerged. It suggested a different world, maybe one without slaves or black people or the white people's unearned and unwarranted privilege and arrogance or a world where all of that existed together.

In reality, referring to them as Dexter's people didn't really illustrate his disapproval of the entire slavery enterprise. Treating them with respect within the boundary that slavery demanded wasn't enough either. Having family members, who declared their intolerance for slavery many years ago, almost from the very beginning, didn't seem to have had any impact. The reality of an unknown unpredictable change, one that his family had once vigorously advocated, was on its way.

Some folks, even some of his people, thought it kind of odd that Mr. Dexter, especially when he became really sickly and frail, would not allow his wife to assume the management of the Manor. Maybe it was because she was not a Princeton, except through marriage, and would not understand the dynamics of the family's history, especially since the colony had become a nation. Mr. Dexter was the first and the last Princeton to live a set of ideals, which didn't address the slavery issue. There would be no others. Madie Marie and he were childless.

He had often thought about Madie Marie and himself and, of course, Christopher, and wished things had been different. Sometimes, he would think of Chris as their own child, dreaming of a night when Madie Marie and he would have made passionate love and Chris would have been conceived. But there wasn't ever such a night or day, ever. It was only a dream. There were, in reality, only nights of long quiet darkness and yearning.

When he brought Madie Marie home as his wife, the plantation community went into shock. They were disappointed he hadn't chosen one of them. After all, they knew him and his family lore. While many didn't know how old he was, a few did remember when he arrived from England. They knew he was a heck of a lot older than his new wife. When together, standing next to each other, they looked like father and daughter, rather than husband and wife.

She couldn't have been much more than eighteen or nineteen years old when they married. There would have been a few eligible young white ladies available and in pursuit of Dexter, had it been known that he liked younger, much younger women. There were some daughters about Miss Madie Marie's age, but none as pretty or enticing or exciting. They all thought Miss Madie Marie was far more mature than her tender age suggested. She acted all grownup-like and talked that way too. Of course, she was a Northerner.

And when Mr. Dexter brought home this very young, frail, almost dead baby shortly after he arrived with her as his wife several weeks later, well, the place exploded with rumors, sly remarks, probing eyes, and forbidden looks.

Some wondered if she had given birth and hid the poor thing somewhere until she could convince Dexter to retrieve it. Others thought the best thing to do was to just stay out of it and see what the Princeton family did. It had a certain reputation to maintain, and Mr. Dexter was very much a Princeton.

It wasn't the stories about that baby, Christopher. It was what Madie Marie called him that got Dexter's attention. It was the fact that Madie Marie was getting attached to him. Anyone could have knocked on their door and claim him and have that piece of paper to prove it.

That's the way it was. A piece of paper could determine ownership of another person. And as Christopher grew into a fine specimen of a man, handsome and muscular, Madie Marie's attachment grew.

The few who had seen him said he wasn't white for sure.

In their minds, he was colored and a slave. End of story!

Mr. Dexter wanted to conclude that just because Christopher had some color in his skin that didn't automatically make him a slave. There was a law that said a child was whatever his mother was, no matter the skin color. If Christopher's mother had been a white woman, he wasn't a slave. Mr. Dexter had said that to several other plantation owners, and they had looked at him and laughed.

Christopher was a mystery. Of course, it was only a topic of interest when Mr. Dexter took him to town and others saw him. Their imaginations ran shamelessly and they would say things or ask awkward questions. But there were also those who remembered when Mr. Dexter discovered that little baby boy on that bench but seldom mentioned it. He was a Princeton and that came with a legendary reputation.

Mr. Dexter had just had his people transfer his cotton, corn, hemp, and timber to the Short Line Railroad cars. Its cars ran eight miles from Fourpoint City to the pier where the big slave powered rowboats would then carry everything to the big steam-driven riverboat anchored in the Mississippi River.

On his way to the only tavern in Fourpoint City, Mr. Dexter had seen this little bitty baby lying on a bench all by itself. It looked awful. Its eyes were all puffy and teary, and dried mucus covered his nose and the left side of his face. The rag around its bottom was full and stinky. The baby's crying was so weak that one could hardly hear it or could easily choose not to. Either way, the baby was just there, trying hard to breath. Everyone walked right past that little snotty-nosed thing and simply ignored its wimpy noise, except Mr. Dexter Princeton.

Mr. Dexter, along with his wife, Madie Marie, was known to be too indulgent and accommodating to most people they encountered, especially their people. It was part of the Princeton family legacy. When no one came to see about it, Mr. Dexter picked the baby up and took it to see old Doc. Jansen. Doc. promptly told him the baby was colored, and about eighteen months old, and would be dead before daybreak, and the best thing he could do was take it back to where he found it. Maybe somebody would claim it or throw it in the river, after it dies, of course. And Dexter did just that. He took it back to the bench and left it, thinking, hoping someone would claim it before he left town.

He then went about his usual Fourpoint City routine. He had a meal with drinks at the tavern, which sometimes included dining with the other slave owners. And then he paid his usual visit to the colored girls' brothel. This was his way of showing respect to his family's heritage. No one in his family had ever indulged in the sexual privileges that were their assumed right as slave owners, at least, as far as he knew. As a matter of fact, one of his ancestors may have actually opened the first colored girls' brothel in town to address that apparent indulgence.

As the story goes, when no one claimed the baby, Dexter took the little fellow home with him. Madie Marie had him cleaned up by the maid, named him Christopher and then fell in love with him.

Since Madie Marie didn't have any children, Christopher had stayed in the house with her and consumed most of her time, almost like he was her child. He used to crawl around the house and hide under her dress. What he saw or smelled under there was anybody's guess. Her visitors, who were few, were highly alarmed. Some were offended, but she didn't really care. And Mr. Dexter seemed more embarrassed than angry. But when he learned that little Christopher often bathed with her until he was a teenager, and during those years, he would sit on a box and keep her company, often washing her back, when he learned this, Mr. Dexter became really concerned and told her so.

Her explanation was that it was better for him to see her naked than go after some other white woman he didn't know and really get in trouble. This, of course, sent various images through Dexter's mind. Especially disturbing was the image of Christopher's hands touching parts of her porcelain body that he assumed were only for his hands.

What they did when Mr. Dexter was not around was a mystery to him. But because there were no babies coming from her, half-white or otherwise, and the townsfolk and the other plantation owners didn't talk about them, he felt more comfortable. But his suspicion and imagination remained quite active and disturbing.

Everybody knew about Lillie Lee, because she was so different from the other female slaves. She didn't look like the others or carry herself like them. Her mother had been one of Mr. Dexter's earlier relative's favorite house servants. Her father was unknown, at least that's what folk said. One plantation owner named Franklin Slayton said she had the features of an Indian with those high cheekbones and long, thick black hair, and the body structure of a young African female, tall and lissome and strong-looking, but she also had blue eyes, thin lips, and a golden skin color, different but really beautiful, especially in the sun light. In Mr. Dexter's mind, she and Christopher would make the best kind of breeding, and not only because of the way their children would look.

But Zachary, who owned the plantation southwest of the Princeton Manor, really wanted Lillie Lee. Dexter had to tell him she wasn't for sale many times, but he would always ask. Zachary had mixed feelings about Dexter. On the one hand, Dexter never laughed at his speech impediment; but on the other, he was that uppity Dexter Princeton who called his place the Manor and he had that gal he wanted, Lillie Lee.

"Wha-what about tha-that golden gal you got, fellow?" Every time Zachary saw Dexter, he would ask this question in the same way. It was either Mr. Fellow at the opening of his question or fellow at the end. He knew, of course, this would irritate Dexter.

"Fellow! I've told you many times. I'm Mr. Princeton to the likes of you!"

"You-you ain't no Mis-Mister to me. And-and Princeton don't mean nothing to me. You-you'll see-see one day."

Zachary's slaves made fun of him when he wasn't around because he was short, ugly, and bald, but having the same first and last name made him even funnier. His slaves would mimic his mother calling him, Zac, Zacha, Zachary, or something like that. Anyway, they had lots of fun with it when he wasn't around.

Zachary had told Dexter he should put Lillie Lee in the colored gals' brothel and make lots of money or have babies with her himself. Dexter ignored him, of course.

There were many stories about where Lillie Lee came from. That's how different she looked and acted. One of Zachary's slaves said he was the first one to see her. She had just appeared around midnight, fully-grown and beautiful, and had asked him if she was in Nashville. Of course, each time he told the story he added more and more, like he said he was standing out in the field when she dismounted from a flying black stallion that had floated down to earth on a white cloud.

Lillie Lee was well aware of her eminence in the community, but it frightened her and she felt exposed to the yearning of all kinds of unsavory characters. So, she looked to Mr. Dexter and Christopher as saviors and was more than willing to hide away in Christopher's shack, hoping he would protect her.

During the early 1860s, around the time when folks were just hearing about the Dred Scott Case and the abolitionist attacks, especially the John Brown raids, there was a lot of fear and confusion among the small community of plantation owners that depended on the railroad at Fourpoint City.

There were lots of unknowns, especially with the possibility of slavery ending. South Carolina was also trying to encourage the Southern states to abandon the Union with all its talk about liberty for all and its abolitionist clamor.

And then there was the potential fighting that could include slaves and ex-slaves with rifles fighting for the Union side. The Confederate had assumed slaves, ex or otherwise, would never fight against their masters.

Everybody at Fourpoint City knew that the South would be nothing without its slaves. Some even concluded the Union with all its abolitionist talk would also be nothing without slavery. Slavery made the Union wealthy and gave it world prominence sooner than anyone expected.

It also made a lot of undistinguished and common white men wealthy and powerful with land and slaves and gave them a taste and desire for aristocratic superiority at any cost. But Dexter's family was already wealthy, already felt superior and it was a family tradition to think slavery was temporary.

But for the other plantation owners, who brought their goods to Fourpoint City, slavery was not temporary. For them, it was the essence of their lives, sanctioned by God and provided substance and prosperity for their families and the nation's future. But they knew, could feel it in their bones that change was coming. They just didn't know how or what it would be or when.

Zachary Zachary, however, knew exactly what he was going to do. When he felt really threatened, his plan was to march all of his slaves, along with the ones he could steal, to Texas, with the idea of taking them into Mexico and joining the territory he had heard would become a slave nation.

Fourpoint City was a far cry from a slave nation. The city was really nothing more than the railroad track, a tavern, a post office, a colored gals' brothel, a little house where three white prostitutes lived and worked, and Nightingale's little church house up the road a piece.

Although the four plantations, Princeton Manor, Franklin Slayton, Phillip Nightingale, and Zachary Zachary plantations covered a lot of acreage, they all came together at Fourpoint City.

The railroad company insisted on owning the land alongside the track on both sides, forming a U-shaped road for the loading and unloading of the wagons. The train made one trip each way twice a month during harvesting time and once a month otherwise. It would arrive in Fourpoint City early in the morning, usually around seven, and leave for its trip back to the Pier midafternoon, around three. There were four freight cars, one for each plantation and the Manor. So, the engine pushed the cars into the city and pulled them out of the city.

The day that everybody remembered, slaves and owners alike, was one of those clear autumn mornings that ended the hot agony of summer with the dreadful sight of clothesline after clothesline with hanging pieces of raggedy shirts and dresses and plain old rags stretched across the yards of the slave shacks.

Mr. Dexter had been sick with the consumption, but he remembered that morning well because he woke up feeling more energetic than usual. And he knew he would need all the energy he could muster. The time had come for him to get his people to load everything they had harvested onto wagons, travel to the city, and load everything onto his railroad car for its trip down to the

Pier. Madie Marie had suggested that Christopher take the wagon to the city, but Mr. Dexter had said no. That was his responsibility.

So waking up that morning feeling a bit more energetic was a big deal for him. He could take the trip to the city with his people and feel decent maybe. Christopher, he decided, would need to go with him. Mr. Dexter wanted him to learn this part of Manor operations. Usually, Christopher would stay behind and work in the wood shop or help Miss Madie Marie and, if need be, protect her from unsavory characters that might pass through.

Mr. Dexter had been getting weaker, losing weight, coughing, and spitting up blood. That was another reason for Christopher to travel with him. He would know what to do if he got sick and protect him, if necessary.

Miss Madie Marie was disturbed and spent sleepless nights because of Mr. Dexter's night sweats, coughing, restlessness, and propensity to release gas, which filled the air with a foul odor. Hearing him hacking, spitting up blood, and farting during the night was more than she wanted or could bear. The thought did occur to her several times that whatever he had might be contagious. She moved downstairs into a quieter bedroom, one she had used occasionally for her own private moments. She convinced him it was a necessary move. Often Mr. Dexter had been too miserable to protest.

But on that morning, he had told her to be ready because when he returned, he would be. There was a sparkle in his eyes. He had smiled. She had smiled too, knowing nothing would happen.

On that day, Mr. Dexter and his wagons were the first ones to arrive, which was actually easier, especially since his railroad car was always the first one in and the last one out. It meant that if the other planters arrived at the same time, the dusk could be unbearable for Mr. Dexter.

That day, after the dust had settled and Mr. Dexter's coughing had become less frequent, all the planters gathered to look for the smoke from the engine, except there was no smoke! No engine either! Nothing! Mr. Dexter started walking toward the tavern and the other planters followed. Maybe, he thought, it had been delayed for some unforeseen reason.

While they often insisted on sitting at the same table, they didn't talk much. That seemed to be okay with them, even if they spent their time looking around the room, out the window, and down at the floor, anything to avoid looking and talking to each other.

There was, however, an unusual connection among them that day, a strange energy that felt a lot like uncertainty, fear, and anxiety. They looked at each other but said nothing.

There had been many rumors about the Union soldiers headed their way, maybe slowing or cutting all transportation south. Maybe their train had to wait for the boat to arrive from up north somewhere. Even if they were just rumors, they were strong enough to be somehow reflected on their faces. They waited and hoped.

Then there was another rumor that no one wanted to talk about, which involved the railroad bosses building a set of tracks north of them. For what, they didn't know.

"I...I wonder what don...done happened to ourrrr train?" It was Zachary Zachary talking, not to anyone in particular, just talking, nervous talking. His speech problems would become worse, especially if there was any kind of crisis that affected him. So, he would try to talk a lot slower, like he needed to focus more. That day, however, it really didn't matter.

Everyone was thinking about the absent train in his own way. Franklin pulled softly on his bread. Phillip looked upward and seemed to be mumbling to himself. Dexter stared at the floor. And Zachary talked. No one looked his way. They didn't like him much. He wasn't pleasant to look at or be around and was known for always having an answer, right or wrong, stuttering or not, regardless of the subject.

"Maybe th...them damn Union so...soldiers don-done taken o...over the river. I bet that's what don...done happened." He was clearly getting excited and had started to push his chair back from the table as if he were about to get up.

"Just hold on there, Zac," Rev. Phillip Nightingale said. He was the only minister for miles. He had his slaves build the church down the road from the tavern. No one attended but him, his family, and his slaves, who had to sit in the back, away from his family or any other white person.

"What's th...that you call me? Donnn't be...be ca...calling me that. You don't kn...know me that way." Zachary stood up and looked at Phillip who looked away.

It was probably a good thing the railroad man burst through the door with such force that everybody in the tavern looked his way suddenly. Whatever Zachary was about to do or say ended suddenly.

"Well, yawl knows me! I ain't got time for no talking or discussion here. Listen good, so I won't have to repeat myself. I got to move on down the road. Them gals waiting for me!"

"The big railroad men want me to tell yawl there won't be no more trains running to Fourpoint City from the pier. That's it, unless yawl pitch in and buy the train and the track, everything. They say they will kick in the upkeep of the engine. That's all! And when the time comes, they're willing to talk about cost but not now. They too busy! That's it! When this quiet down, then they will talk.

"I tell you something else. It's a mess, everywhere! I know! I go all over for the railroad. I seed some stuff, I tell you! Mens killing each other, white men. All 'cause niggers don't want to be niggers anymore. What they gon' be? Niggers! They just be running loose all over the place. Who gon' get them niggers back where they belong?

"I tell you something else, ain't supposed to, but I will. If yawl was to start growing corn, foodstuff like that, them railroad men might have a change of heart. Cotton ain't king no more.

"Something else, they planning on building some tracks up north, not far from here. Fact is, they planning on building tracks all over. Hey, I got to go. I got these gals waiting for me." He left, closing the door loudly behind him.

They all looked at each other, except Dexter who continued to look at the floor. Zachary quickly turned away and looked directly at Dexter.

"Tell you...tell you on...one thing. I'll tak...take that gal, Lillie Lee, off your hands. Rig...right now! That one yo...you won't nee...need to be con...concern about."

Dexter, who had not said a word or reacted to the railroad man's message, stood up, looked at each of them, and walked out of the tavern, closing the door softly behind him.

"See, see! That damn Dexter! He just up...up and walk...walked out. No discussion, no nothing! See, see, that bastard thin...think he's bet...better than us. I'll show him. I kno...know what I nee...need to do. For me! Bes-

best yawl dooo the sa...same." With that, Zachary stormed out of the tavern.

The wind was high and everything outside was chaotic. The slaves were in mindless motion, moving here and there, trying to keep everything in order, and listening for the train's whistle. Mr. Dexter had ordered his people to turn the wagons around and head back to the manor.

The wind swirled and whirled, gathering and spreading dust and causing Mr. Dexter to cough and spit up blood. Clearly, he was growing weaker and weaker. Christopher with the help of Mr. Dexter's people had to put him gently on the bed of the lead wagon. It was then that Mr. Dexter began to realize that he would have to depend on Christopher more than he ever thought.

Rev. Phillip Nightingale stood at the tavern door, smiling, confident that everything before him was in God's hands. He was convinced that it was part of His great master plan. It was a proud moment for Rev. Nightingale. His Lord was about to show everyone his love and kindness. And he would be elevated to His Lord's main disciple. The victory was at hand. His slaves, however, waited, obviously nervous and impatient and seemingly in fear, except some of them seemed emboldened. The grapevine had brought them a message too.

Mr. Dexter had heard Rev. Nightingale's Christian predictions and assertions before. But he was Dexter Princeton. A Christian! But also, a very different kind of Christian. He always knew and felt confident that slavery would end, now or later. There was never any doubt. Christianity didn't need to teach him that.

The Princeton's bloodline in the new nation was ending. Sometimes, he agonized over that, and then sometimes he didn't. How, he sometimes thought, could I leave the Princeton Manor without a Princeton leader?

There were other times, however, when he was satisfied that the Princeton legacy could end with him, and the family could be proud. Because if slavery was to end, the Princeton family could say they were always uncomfortable with the way slaves were treated. They could say they never used the word slave or slavery.

Since England had denounced slavery years ago, the family felt it had to follow suit. After all, the family's legacy dated back to the exploits of the Crusades. Of course, because the profits were good, extremely good, the family back in England was comfortable waiting for the end to come. It could then return to the business of searching for gold and silver.

As he lay there on the bed of his wagon, he wondered if all his relatives before him had really believed that slavery would end. And when it didn't, what did they think or do? He thought he knew the answer. Slavery became black gold. And Princeton Manor still existed because they made their slaves their people and treated them differently.

Mr. Dexter had wanted to talk to Madie Marie about the future of Princeton Manor, should something happen to him. He wanted to think about that conversation first, but each time, the image of Christopher would be somewhere in his mind's eye. He couldn't separate them, and he couldn't think of himself without Christopher being at his side or somewhere in the picture.

He had to admit to himself that he had been jealous of Christopher's relationship with Madie Marie. There had never been any real tangible evidence that there was anything more than a caring relationship between them, at least that was all he knew. But sometimes his imagination would get the best of him, thus the pictures he created in his mind of Christopher satisfying her needs.

She was nineteen-years or so older than Christopher, and Dexter was twenty years or so older than she. She was still beautiful and desirable and still had needs that he didn't think he fulfilled. It was his imagination inserting itself into his reality that created problems for him and often made him worry.

Madie Marie was experiencing her daily frustration with learning to crochet when she heard the commotion out front and assumed Chris and Dexter and his people were returning from Fourpoint City. It was strange, however, because she didn't expect them back until nightfall. It did disturb her a bit that this time, he had taken Christopher with him, leaving her alone and, consequently, unprotected.

Her first thought, of course, was for Dexter, who spent most days and nights in bed, except when he was actually having a good day. She tried deliberately not to worry too much. Christopher, who was always assuming more and more Manor responsibilities, was with him.

She had leisurely walked to the door leading to the little porch off the kitchen, comfortable that if there were a problem, Dexter or Christopher would certainly handle it as always.

When she got to the door, she found Dexter's people walking away from the wagon but looking back at Christopher who was standing at its rear gate, looking abandoned.

"Chris! What's happened? Where is Dexter?" No one called him Chris but her. To everyone else, he was Christopher.

"Here, he's here. Come!" Christopher beckoned for her to join him. When she did she found Dexter lying helpless and motionless on the bed of the wagon.

"Is he . . . ?"

"No, no. He's just sleep or something, I think. His coughing may have been too much."

"Why did everyone walk off? Surely, they don't think I will hold them responsible?"

"I know you haven't heard yet, but the railroad's not running to Fourpoint City anymore. And the grapevine is, the news is slavery is over. Many, some slaves are leaving, running to the Union lines. They are also killing their owners, if they have to."

"We don't have slaves, Chris. You know that. We never treat our people as slaves, you know, the way others do. So . . ." It was like a light went off in her head. "They really think they should be like us, me and Mr. Dexter. And you, of course! Why shouldn't they be? I agree with them. And . . . and I think Mr. Dexter would too. Don't you? Like Mr. Dexter, I mean." She was clearly struggling to understand what was happening.

"Yeah, I think so, I guess."

"Chris, you should tell them it's not what they think. Me and Mr. Dexter . . . "

"They know about you and Mr. Dexter. They also know about me. How you kept me in the house with you when I was little, slept in your bed. You and Mr. Dexter taught me to read and do numbers and helped me, made me the man I am. Strong and...a man! You did! They know I'm not like them. But I'm not like you either. I know that."

She looked at him like she was seeing him for the first time. "I've . . . Dexter and me always treated you like you were one of us."

"But I'm not."

"Get someone to help us with him." She stepped back, away from the wagon.

Christopher jumped onto the wagon and grabbed Mr. Dexter shoulders, "Just grab his feet. We can do this."

"No, you go get someone to help us. Surely, there is someone."

After Christopher left, she took a seat in her white rocker on the little porch, the one that Christopher made, where she and Mr. Dexter and Christopher spent many pleasant hours sipping tea and talking.

She remembered telling him, maybe for the first times in Mr. Dexter's presence, that slavery would not last forever and how it made her feel. She was proud and confident, sitting right there on that porch in that same chair with her head high, knowing she was right.

But she hadn't stopped to think about what that would mean for her and people like her who had depended on their slaves for practically everything, planting and harvesting, cooking and cleaning, standing and waiting, everything, especially that feeling of superiority and privilege.

And with Mr. Dexter lying there helpless, she realized she had no idea what would happen to her. All her relatives were up north, and he had none in this country.

She stood up quickly and looked to see if Chris was returning with the help needed to carry Mr. Dexter into the house where he could tend to his illness. He was nowhere in sight. But, Mr. Dexter had started to cough again and move his arms in an effort to get up.

She didn't hesitate. She moved as quickly as she could to the wagon, only to discover she couldn't reach him, couldn't help him get up unless she was able to get up into the wagon with him.

She stood there, reaching for him, realizing that he was all she had.

"Let me help you, miss." He was covered with dust so thick that she didn't notice his grey jacket or his missing arm. He moved quickly from his horse to the ground to the wagon and to her side. "Where your niggers at? They ought to be here doing this."

"I'm sorry, but we don't call our people that! And thank you, but help is on the way." She had stepped back, away from the man to get a good look at his face and to get away from his smell. She frowned, repelled by his scars and his rugged skin and intrusive odor.

"Don't let my face scare you none. I'm as gentle as a lamb. 'Course, ain't no lambs around here, I 'pect. These are all battle wounds from up there in Nashville. And they remind me every day what it means to be a Southern gentleman. My name is Chester. Let me help you some here. Then, maybe you can help me."

Mr. Dexter had fallen back to his prior position, but he appeared to be trying desperately to get Miss Madie Marie's attention.

"Thank you, but we can manage. Is it food you want? Just go around to the back, and someone will bring you something." But she realized there was no one to do that, and the thought frightened her.

"No, don't need no food, Missus. Shot me a rabbit the other day. Little-bitty thing but cooked up real good, ought to last me a day or two. My old grandpa, he told me before I left from down home with the Rebel soldiers that I had a cousin up around these parts somewhere. Couldn't think of his name, but he was close around some place called Fourpoint City.

"Y'all know where that is? Grandpa told me to look him up if I ever had a chance, 'cause wasn't many of us left, family, I mean. And since the fighting been going the way it is, probably even less. All my folks, the ones I know of, they down around the eastern part of Mississippi, near Macon. Right there near the Alabama state line. Heck some of my folks was born in Alabama, I think. Probably on my mama's side. They all left the homestead, figuring they would get their own place with niggers and all, and do all right. He, my grandpa, he didn't know if they did or not. They were supposed to, according to him.

"Now this cousin what's around here, my grandpa said, he was my mother's sister's son's son on that side of the family. He said he didn't know much about my daddy's side. Hell, you could be on that side of the family as far as I know, 'cept you a heap bit too pretty and refined, I 'pect. Anyway, this cousin done all right for himself, at least grandpa thought he did. He got lots of land and a whole bunch of niggers . . . slaves, I mean.

"Grandpa couldn't remember his own cousin's name. Heck, he can't remember what happened yesterday. 'Course he ain't seed him since, this cousin person, I mean, well, hell, he was real little, my cousin, I mean, so I don't know why he thought he would remember his name," he paused, looking at Miss Madie Marie with a huge grin on his face. "Don't mind me none. Let me get up in this wagon. They always said I talk too much. I don't mind being told to hush up."

"Hush up. Please! Look, Chris will be here soon to help me. He'll be fine till then. If you go around . . . " she paused, and he spoke up.

"To the back? Well, heck, missus, niggers go to the back door, not white men like me. Heck, if we ain't careful, they all be coming in the front door. Plus, I know how to act in the front parlor of a big house. What you think, I grew up in one of them tin roof shacks? I know my house manners pretty good. Hell, before I lost this arm, there was some talk about making me an officer. I know how to conduct myself around the high up people." He was becoming agitated, but he was smiling.

"Just help me get him out of the wagon. Then I'll give you directions to Fourpoint City."

The soldier couldn't pick up Dexter or carry him or do much of anything with one arm. He could hardly get up into the wagon. He and Miss Madie Marie pushed and pulled Dexter to the edge of the wagon. Dexter never opened his eyes or coughed or anything. He almost fell off the wagon twice, but they finally eased him to the ground. This was as far as she wanted to go. She didn't want the stranger on her porch or in her house. Other than Chris, she had never been in the company of another man, except her husband, Dexter, and her cousin.

"Thank you. I can make it from here. Fourpoint City isn't far from here, can't miss it. When you see this road, well, it's really not a road. It's more like a way of going, a trail like. Take that all the way around until you get there, to the city. Just keep on that trail. There will be fresh wagon tracks. Just follow them. They'll take you straight to where you want to go. You should know there's talk about the Yankee soldiers headed in this direction, but you'll be safe there, most likely. Clean up a bit. Folks might think you deserted or something."

"That way, huh? That's going toward the river, ain't it? I always did want to see that big old river. What they call it? The Mighty Mississippi. Guess now is as good a time as any."

"Yes, thank you. Here is a fifty-cent piece, and it's not Confederate money. It'll get you whatever you want."

"Well now, you don't have to do that. The Lord, he knows I tried to help out as best I can. Done given a lot for his cause. My arm here is gone. 'Course now, he done gave me a lot too. Grandpa use to tell me the Lord had something special for me. I just needed to wait, you know.

That's the hard part, waiting. But I can feel it in my bones. It ain't gon' be too long.

"I always try to be good to folks. Grandpa said that was the one thing he loved to do. Now that's the Lord's work. He gave us so much, the Lord did. We ought to be thankful. Them folks up north, they just don't know. They just don't know."

"You go on now; he'll be okay. I will too. Our people are on their way." She watched him as he rode off, thinking he might have waved if he had two arms. There was still the task of getting Dexter onto the porch, in the house, up the stairs, and into his room.

She had to wait for Chris or maybe one of her people who should be around the house somewhere anyway. Someone was always there somewhere doing something. Mr. Dexter had insisted on it. They were the house people, and she depended on them to be there for her every need. That, after all, was their only responsibility.

She knew they all loved her. And she loved them, in her own way. She was nice to them and even gave her old clothes to Lillie Lee. She once gave a pair of new red bloomers to her. She had thought them a bit risqué for her taste. They were a gift from Dexter, but she never could bring herself to wear them. She thought Lillie Lee would.

She was convinced Dexter and she had always done the right things for her people, more than any of the other owners. And with her prediction coming true, the one about slavery ending, she wondered why she wasn't happy.

It was the right thing to do; at least she had been brought up to think that way. Her mother had stressed the immorality of treating people as slaves. Her father, a successful businessman, was often silent on the question of slavery but agreed on several occasions, especially at church.

She knew slavery was wrong anyway, except now that she was directly benefiting from it, she wondered what she would do without it.

The privileges that came with it had become a way of life, and she would have to give that up. It didn't matter how well she treated their people. She and Dexter would most likely have to pay for that lifestyle.

She also had to think about Chris.

"Madie, Madie Marie, help me stand up! I need to get in bed and just rest for a while. Don't worry. I'll be okay." Mr. Dexter's coughing and the blood coming out of his mouth, mixed with mucus and phlegm, along with the difficulty he was having breathing and the teary eyes were all too much for her. Just too much, especially when he would reach out for her!

"Help me!"

She just stood, frozen there, not really knowing what to do. The daily, intimate realities of her husband's illness were the responsibilities of their people. She didn't even know the range of his illness or what it was. All she knew was what she was told by them. She stood there as he reached for her help.

There were no doctors nearby. As a matter of fact, she didn't know where the nearest doctor was. She did know, however, about the old slave on the Franklins' place who knew all about roots and herbs and voodoo with special spirits. But she could never resort to that. She was a Christian.

She had left an affluent life living with her parents where she always had things done for her by servants to a life with Dexter and his people who also did everything for her. She suddenly realized she had always lived with other people doing for her, never having to do for herself. She had never thought about her Dexter ever wanting anything or in need of anything, because their people had always been there to help, to give. But there he was, on the ground, behind his wagon, still reaching for her help. It wasn't a shock, but a sudden abrupt realization that she was alone, all alone, without protection or assistance. All she could do, all she was prepared to do, was watch her Dexter reach for her. She couldn't move. Standing there looking at him made her realize just how addicted she had become to always having someone there to do for her.

"Okay, all right, as soon as someone gets here. Chris went to get some help."

"They are all gone, aren't they? My people, I mean? I had a feeling when the railroad man said . . . " Dexter's eyes seemed to go blank.

"Shhhh, don't try to talk." She knew as much as he did about what was going on.

Chris had already told her. He thought what she had hoped for was going to come true. Slavery would soon be over. She looked at her Dexter whose eyes had gone blank, and her tears ran freely.

"I don't know what to do." She ran to the edge of the porch and looked around. "Chris will be here soon. He'll know."

But her Dexter had stopped reaching.

She wanted to scream for help, but there was no one who would hear her, no one. The Manor was located far enough from the county road that a scream wouldn't be heard nor could the Manor be seen unless there was a deliberate effort. That was the way Dexter wanted it, and he felt safe living with his people.

While the other plantation owners lived in fear because they were outnumbered, Dexter had never felt fear, not that kind of fear. For Madie Marie, it wasn't fear either. It was disappointment, in Dexter and herself, especially herself. She never intended to get so comfortable with slavery. But year after year, they both grew more and more comfortable.

She crumbled to the ground beside Dexter. It was a strange realization. She had never thought their lives would end with such overwhelming sorrow. She thought she wanted, needed, to hold him, to feel his warmth next to her, but she didn't reach for him or make any move to touch him. She just looked at him and knew his warmth was gone. Forever.

She sat there, alone, tears in her eyes as she looked out at the early signs of a beautiful moonlit evening. She could have gotten up and sat in her chair and been comfortable, but she wanted to be near him. She sat there until Christopher returned with the news that no one was coming.

"No one is coming? Why? After we treated them like real people? No one is coming?"

"I'm here."

"But you're not . . . the help we need." She wanted to say 'one of them' but paused, looking away from him. "I . . . we need more than just you and me. And . . . and what took you so long? I don't know what to do. We need to get him upstairs to his bed." She thought she wanted, needed, to be firm, sound firm, at least. But she couldn't, certainly not with Chris.

"I think he's dead, Miss Madie Marie."

"Don't call me Miss! You know I don't like that. You think we can get him up the stairs, just the two of us? Help me up here."

Christopher extended his hand. She clasped it and looked into his face.

"I don't know what I would do without you. How could they not come and help him and me? He was as nice to them as he could be, not like the others owners. I just don't understand." But she held onto his hand even as she stood in front of him.

"Mr. Dexter is dead, Madie Marie." He looked at her, and his look made her nervous.

"Of course, he is. We can't wake him, can we? He's going to need to be dressed differently. I can't undress him. You can, maybe."

"I can't either."

"Isn't it strange? I've lived with him all these years and have never seen him . . . without clothes on. Lord, what am I going to do? Help me here." She was still holding onto Chris's hand. Then without any notice or preparation, she found her arms around him and his around her. And a moment passed and then another, and then she simply collapsed in tears in his arms.

"Maybe we shouldn't have raised you to think you are as good as we are. Then you would be acting differently, maybe not even be here." She carefully removed her arms and stepped back, moving closer to the porch. But she reached for his hand.

Their fingers touched, and he quickly but softly took her hand and moved toward her. "Yeah, I wouldn't be here. I would be gone, heading north, away from folks like you. That's if you had treated me like one of your people!"

"Folk like me, you think we don't know how much better off we are, privileged and all? I know. I really know now." She shook her head vigorously affirming what she had just said. "This is such a lovely porch. It's who we are, the three of us."

"You want the good parts, the benefits, like the porch and what it means to us. It's the other parts you don't want to know about. Don't want to see. And you didn't. Mr. Dexter saw to that. Here at the Manor, you had only the best part," he paused and looked at her.

Suddenly, she tried to become more businesslike. "I don't have time for this, Chris. You know who we are, me and Mr. Dexter. You have always known. Now, it's just me. And you. Maybe that's the way it ought to be."

"Maybe, but I didn't have a choice, did I? Now I do. Now I do, Madie Marie. For the first time, I have a choice. But I don't know where that choice will take me."

She looked at him, and somewhere she found the strength to stand her ground. "Yes, you do! And what is it? Are you apart of us, me and Dexter? I know the answer, Chris! Otherwise, you wouldn't have come back."

He looked at her, and she touched his cheek softly. She knew her touch would keep her Chris beside her.

"Mr. Dexter had me build five coffins last week. We took all of them to the train but one. It's in the shed. The others are still on one of the wagons." He remembered how as a little boy, he would follow Mr. Dexter around and how he would have skilled tradesmen teach him to build things, do specialized work. That's where he had learned his carpentry skills, where he learned to build coffins and anything else his eyes could see.

Mr. Dexter had told Christopher they should always have several coffins on hand. Sometimes slave owners would bury their good slaves in coffins, and sometimes they would just throw them in a hole up at the slave burial pit. Christopher spent at least two days a week making plain coffins.

He also built fancy ones for the white folks. Mr. Dexter told him when he wasn't building or repairing something around the plantation, he should be making coffins, the fancy six-sided ones.

That day when Mr. Dexter took Madie Marie and him across the yard was fresh in his mind. It was a really hot day, sticky and uncomfortable for all of them, especially Madie Marie.

"I'm gon' burn up out here, Dexter. You know I don't like all this blazing sun on me. Change my complexion, you know. I'll be looking like one of our people or peeling like an apple before long. We could be sitting on Chris's little porch in the shade drinking a cold glass of lemonade. There's always a nice breeze there," she'd spoken in her most affected Southern drawl. She was laughing, holding her widest summer hat on her head as if it were windy. Both Mr. Dexter and Christopher had the same unspoken thought at the same time.

"See that little plot of land I had set off with little sticks? That's where the family burial plot is going to be. Look, you will be able to see it from our bedroom window. We'll always be in view of each other."

"This is just too morbid for me. I'll be on the porch in the shade. Y'all can tell me about it, honey." She laughed and walked away saying, "Dexter, whatever possess you to think about something like this."

They watched her sashay across the yard with one hand on her hip and the other holding the hat on her head. They were both smiling, thinking how beautiful she looked even with just seeing her back. But when they turned back to the matter at hand, their smiles were gone.

"I had planned it for the family, but it doesn't seem like there will be one, except us. I . . . I guess that makes a family, us, since we been together for so long. What I'm saying is . . . you know, most . . . nobody accepts us as a family but us. That's what I'm saying. So, we need to get some wood and paint, white paint, and build a little fence with an opening so someone can walk in," he chuckled to himself. "I haven't the slightest idea who they will be."

Building a short fence and painting it white around this family burial place had been an experience Christopher hadn't enjoyed. Mr. Dexter had watched, smiling, encouraging, and teasing as he walked around the plot. "You know, Christopher, you will probably be the one to bury me and Miss Madie Marie. Right here! There's a spot for you, but don't count on it. These people won't think that was right. But it's there anyway, waiting."

Christopher wanted to respond with his own perceptions but said nothing, didn't even look up.

Where will I be buried, he wondered. In the slaves' graveyard or with the only family I have ever known? He knew the answer.

She stood tall with her head up, as usual. "Get the box, Chris! I told Dexter he shouldn't have you making coffins for dead people. You know what he said? He said somebody had to do it. That man!"

" You know, Chris, it's only you and me now, just the two of us. We'll be alone in the house, just the two of us."

"The coffin is heavy."

"I'll help you. But you know, I need you now more than ever. We'll bury him up in the plot. I will miss him, you know."

"Yes, I know." He looked at her as if she should have said something else, but he didn't know what.

"Can you make a headstone? I'll have to get a proper one, but in the meantime . . . with letters and all."

"What do you want it to say?"

"I don't know." And then, she started crying, uncontrollably crying.

Christopher put his arms around Madie Marie and held her close, so close he thought she could feel him against her.

But she didn't withdraw.

They buried Dexter in the family plot. There was no service, no preacher, nothing, just the two of them. She stood and watched, tearing up occasionally, while Christopher dug the hole and struggled to slide the coffin in and replace the dirt. And a few days later he placed the headstone, which said: MR. DEXTER PRINCETON. That was all.

Life, of course, didn't ever return to normal or at least back to the way they thought it had been. Mr. Dexter's death and his people not doing their daily chores casted a dark, lonely shadow over the activities of the house for several weeks.

During that time, she had insisted that Dexter's room be boarded up, even the window from which that plot of land Chris had designated for family burials could be seen. And he would have accomplished the task with ease except for her insistence that he empty the chamber pot before boarding up the door.

He refused. She didn't know what to do or say to him. There was no command in her voice or whip in her hand. Their history together had eliminated any possible authority she might have had over him. She, after all, had taught him that he was her equal, could turn his back to her, raise his voice, touch her body, and be a man in her presence. That day she had looked at him and seen the man she had created. And she was really pleased. But there was still the issue of the chamber pot.

She didn't know if there was anything in the pot, and neither one of them would look. She decided to have Chris board the door, leaving the room exactly as Mr.

Dexter had left it, bloody sheets and all. As unreasonable as it may seem, she had decided that if the smell became overwhelming, she would move into Christopher's shack and have him build a smaller house for the two of them.

But that was only one of the problems. Christopher was spending more and more time in his shack. Why, she didn't know. She only knew she was being left alone to sit in her rocker, looking out over unruly fields with unwanted shrubs and weeds growing side by side, destroying the work her people had started. And her nights were lonely.

"Why do you leave me each day?" she asked him one day. "What draws you down there? No one is there!"

"You wouldn't understand. Here, let me help you." Chris was gentle, smiling and softly touching her arm. "Come!"

"It's getting so I just can't seem to get to where I want to go. I need you to help me. But you aren't around much. This morning I had a coughing spell, almost passed out."

"Like . . ."

"Don't say it. Wouldn't it be something if we have whatever Dexter had?"

"I didn't sleep with him."

Madie Marie pulls away from Chris. "Oh, I can walk. So, Chris, what's down there? Nothing, right? They're all gone, including Lillie Lee, aren't they? I guess she left with all the others. She did, didn't she?" She looks at him, comfortable that she knew the answer.

"No, not with them, she didn't. She left with that Zachary fellow."

"Zachary? What . . . how did he . . . did she just leave with him? Zachary? I need to sit down for a minute."

"He's taking his slaves to Texas and Mexico to a new kind of slave nation they been talking about. He took her and some of the others with him. Stole them away. I was not there when he took them, or he would not have." The anger swept across Christopher's face.

"But why? What others? They . . . they are all gone, aren't they?"

"No, no one left but the ones he took. They are all waiting. Everybody, including me."

"Waiting for what?" She stopped, shaking her head in disbelief and profound frustration.

"You wouldn't understand. Let me help you to bed. This changes nothing between us. I am still here for you." He was sincere, and she felt it.

"But before you said they were all gone, Chris?"

"Yes, I did."

"You lied to me?"

"Yes, I lied. But lying is all right sometimes. People like me have to lie to keep living."

"But not you. You're like us . . . me. I taught you myself. We don't . . . " and she stopped.

"But you do. Every time I go into town with Mr. Dexter, I am treated like his slave, not his equal. Everyone . . . they all treat me that way, even Mr. Dexter. Why do you think I call him Mr. Dexter? You call him Dexter, like all his equals. I am only like you when I'm with you."

"But you were Dexter's friend."

"Not around them."

"But he didn't even like them. No, I don't understand."

She started coughing but insisted on him helping her to her feet. She was tired all the time, no energy, no explanation. She had always spent her days helping her house people, teaching them how best to serve her and Dexter's needs. But those days were over.

All she did now was sit in that chair and wait for Chris. That was when she noticed a little nagging cough, which seemed to get worse each hour. And it wasn't long before it grew into coughing spells that lasted minutes, an eternity it seemed.

When she started coughing up blood, having night sweats, and losing weight, she knew. But she was still strong enough to have Chris help her to the porch where she would sit, sometimes for hours, waiting for him to return and be with her and help her to bed.

"Have I been blind, Chris? A fool?" Madie Marie asked.

"That's for you to say." He helped her to stand and slowly walked her to her bedroom. At the door, she paused and looked at him.

"Help me to my bed. Get my nightgown. I need you to help me undress."

Sometimes during the night, she heard this hammering. When she turned and looked at her window, Christopher was standing outside, nailing boards across it. He waved at her and smiled. Of course, she yelled for him to stop. He ignored her.

And in the next second, he was nailing boards across her door from the inside. She yelled again for him to stop, and again, he ignored her.

Then, in a flash, he was standing beside her bed, slowly rubbing her arm and telling her softly to relax, to rest, that he was going to stay with her forever. When he said that, the room suddenly became pitch-black. She couldn't see him anymore, but she could feel his presence, his smooth, sensuous rubbing of her arm. She wanted to reach for him and pull him to her, but she couldn't move.

Then he was there beside her in bed. She could feel his presence. She closed her eyes for a second or two, anticipating his next move, his next touch, the touch she had taught him. But nothing happened, no movement, nothing. It was like he was no longer there, but she felt him next to her.

Then there was a light right above her. A startling, brilliant light and the two of them were side by side in midair. And the brilliant light and their images slowly ebbed away into a soft light. It was like her childhood impression of the first snow of the year, the beauty, the peace, the silence, the softness, the stillness, and the threat of imminent danger.

And then she was back on her bed, unable to move, perspiring. Her nightgown clung to her skinny body, her bed was soaking wet. And Chris was no longer there. She knew reality had returned, but she still refused to open her eyes, searching, hoping for that moment to return, but like the first snow of the year, its time had come and gone.

Then she heard the rain and the thunder and felt a strange sensation. She was not alone. Someone was moving around in her room, going through her drawers, searching for something. She knew it wasn't Chris, because there was an urgency about the activity. And Chris had no reason to search for anything because he knew exactly where everything was.

She still had not opened her eyes. She wanted to run her hands quickly over the bed in an effort to find her quilt. But she couldn't move. Then she heard a voice, and her eyes popped wide open.

"You know, I thought you was dead, Cousin." It was Chester!

"They told me back there in that town that Dexter was most likely my cousin. Me and some of them fellows sat in that tavern all day and figured out he could be the only one. Then I went to the preacher man . . . heck, I can't even remember his name, but he seemed like a nice sort. Anyway, he said that was mostly right. You know, y'all was my cousins on my mama's side. I came back here to see y'all and say hello like my grandpa said I should do. He said, 'Chester, when you get there, you be sure and say hello, and you best be polite and all'.

"That's exactly what I done, Cousin Madie Marie. But when I passed y'all's little graveyard and saw that headstone, well, it was all I could do to keep from bursting out in tears. Lord, when did that happen? You know, he didn't look quite right when I last seed him in that wagon, but I didn't know he was that sick. I should have stayed and helped out. That's what I should have done, being my cousin and all. 'Course, I didn't know that then. And Grandpa said he was his only cousin, which made him my only cousin. I sho' hope the good Lord will forgive me for leaving my only cousin, him sick and all."

She wanted to tell him to stop calling her cousin and to hush up but discovered she couldn't. She was horrified by his appearance but couldn't stop looking at him. He looked worse than he did the first time she'd seen him. She was certain if she had been able to smell, she would have been overwhelmed by his odor. And it seemed like with every word he spoke, the room got hotter and hotter, and he wouldn't stop talking.

"And you know what else Grandpa said, Cousin Madie Marie? He used to say this all the time, but I never paid much attention to him. You know how old folk just ramble on about this one thing and another. He said, 'Chester' whenever he would call me like that, I know it's important. I looked right at him so I wouldn't miss a word.

"Now Grandpa, your cousin, had a funny way of saying things. It was like every word came right out of his nose. And Lord, don't let that man catch a cold. You couldn't understand a word he said. I tell you, it was funny.

Anyway, he told me that I was gonna have lots of land with lots of niggers to do my bidding one day. That's what he said. Look what done happened! Ain't that something? The Lord is good, ain't he?

"Heck, that's the way it's supposed to be for people like us in this country. That's why my folks came over here. Didn't have nothing. Nothing. But here I am! Now ain't that something? How did he know? Huh? How?"

She didn't understand what he was talking about and couldn't ask questions. She was helpless and could only think about Chris coming to her aid.

"Tell you what we gone do, Cousin Madie Marie. That was what they said your name was. Anyway, we gon' wait a little while, maybe a day or two, then we'll get married. And I will nurse you back to good health. We'll get married first, then we'll work on your sickness. Cousins do marry, you know. Hell, we may have a baby or two. Maybe a whole bunch!

"You'll be all right, 'cause I know all about being sick and all. Heck, I was in the war. 'Course, now if your niggers got some of their special medicine, heck, I'll have you up and about in no time. Then after that, we'll live happy together forever with all this land and all these niggers to work it. Oh, by the way, where y'all keep the gold and money and stuff like that? What's wrong? Can't you talk? If you can't talk none, don't worry one bit. I'll talk for you. You just rest right now. We'll find everything I need later on."

She was sure he could see the fright in her eyes, but he kept talking, like he was nervous or uncertain about what to do next. And the way he was leering over her weak and sick body frightened her.

"Cousin, you know I ain't had no woman in a long time. The last one was some fat nigger gal. You know something else? I ain't never ever had me a white woman. Never! You know how special this gon' be for me . . . and good! I already know that."

She was shaking her head wildly from side to side. There was just too much going on in her mind, and then he wanted to get in bed with her? She thought she would die first.

"I guess I'll have to do something about these niggers. I know, I know . . . you call them your people. That's okay. But I'll call them my niggers 'cause that's what they is."

He looked away, smiling as if he relished the thought of what he was proposing to do. "Now, I'll need your help here since I don't know them. I guess I'll make that one you call Chris my head nigger. Them boys back in town said he was a good one, just a little bit uppity. Fancy-pants, they called him, said he didn't dress like no slave. That ain't no problem for me. Hell, I'll beat that out of him in no time. And, Cousin Madie Marie, if I need to help you talk, I will! Look at you, lying there and all. I . . . I'm just beside myself. This gonna be real fun! Have us some babies too."

That would never happen. She knew that. Her time was limited. She knew or thought she knew she would be dead soon. Her attention turned to her people. And none of her people had ever been beaten or anything else, certainly not Chris. All she could think about was their not leaving, which she concluded they might regret.

She wanted to tell him no, that her people were never treated that way, especially Chris, but she couldn't even shake her head. All she could manage was to close her eyes several times as quickly as possible. Hopefully, she thought, he would see her anger and protest. But her frustration and fear mounted when she realized her

WITHOUT REDEMPTION

silence to him probably meant she had already given in to his vision of their future.

Then she thought she needed to die even quicker.

"Where he at, this Chris fellow? I need to get things going right away. I'll just go on down there to the slave shacks and get them all to know me as their new master. Ain't that something? Me, a master! Grandpa would be proud of me . . . of us. I will be the big man like I'm supposed to be in no time. They need men like me up here! Them men back at the tavern, there was talking about some folks leaving, going to Texas, Mexico, places like that. Well, I ain't going nowhere! Got me everything I need right here."

He looked at Madie Marie. "I remember how you looked before. I'm gonna have you looking like that again before long. Then it'll be me and you! I just can't wait. You know what? Grandpa was right. The Lord is good! You'll see! Right now, I got some nigger business to take care of. I'll be right back. I'll get my head nigger to tell the others who I am. Kinda announce it, you know? When I get back, we'll see how sick you is."

And he was gone. She wouldn't have heard anything else he said anyway. She had closed her eyes and was waiting, assured that her death was coming soon. Like clockwork, tick tock, tick tock, a mysterious hand waving a magical death wand and spreading its final invisible penetrating dust all over her body, escalating and intensifying her fever, her sweating, and bringing on her final moments. She knew her last moment would be like that first snowfall, beautiful and silent and peaceful and still and deadly. Somewhere in all of this would be the faces of Dexter and Chris, together.

When Chester got to Chris's shack, he found Christopher sitting on his tree stump smiling and chewing on a piece of grass stem. He was far more content than Chester thought a nigger ought to be.

"Hey, boy! You there, can't you hear? Now you know you ain't got no business sitting down in my presence unless I say it's okay. Nigger, get your ass up from there. Ain't gonna tell you again. You gon' be my head nigger! You Chris, ain't you?"

Chris didn't respond or acknowledge his presence.

"Look, nigger, I'm gonna make Chris my head nigger. Is that you? Well, I guess I got to beat some sense in your nappy head first. So y'all will know not to be messing around with me. I ain't playing, boy. I been known to whup a nigger's ass to death. And I ain't lying."

He picked up a piece of board and took three or four menacing steps toward Chris and stopped, realizing, perhaps for the first time, he only had one arm. And Chris's reaction startled him, but he knew he couldn't back down.

Chris did not get up from his stump but looked Chester dead in the eyes, sending so much negative energy toward him that Chester did indeed stop in his tracks.

"There have never been any beatings here, and there never will be. We'll see to that," Christopher said.

"What 'we'? Who that?"

"Miss Madie Marie and me."

"You is Chris. Well, Chris, let me tell you right now. She ain't goin' be seeing to nothing but what I tell her to see to. Hell, I'm the only cousin left, so all of this is gonna be mines, including you and her. You get your black ass over here right now."

There was a long pause. Christopher remained on his tree stump, broke off another piece of grass, and started chewing on it.

"What cousin are you?" he asked. "You don't sound like you anybody's cousin around here, not at Princeton Manor. Mr. Dexter, his folks from England. Been here a long time, from the beginning or close to it. Look at you. You don't look like you're from any place worth anything and don't sound like it either.

"And Madie Marie, she from a fine family from up north. You're nobody's cousin around here, Mister. You do understand that, don't you? You best be getting on your way." Christopher laughed out loud and shook his head. "I better go see about Madie Marie. Here is what you better do, and after that, you best move on. Go on up there to that little clear walking path and put your ear down to the ground. Those sounds you hear are horses headed this way. That's part of General Sherman's Union Army, boys in Blue Coats, and they colored. You know about them, don't you?"

Chester dropped the board as Christopher walked past him. Of course, he knew about them. He had lost his arm fighting them. He smiled because he was told the Rebels won that day. Killed a whole lot of niggers, but they kept on coming. He remembered that too.

"You gonna be surprised when you get up there. And after that, you bring you black ass right on back here. I ain't through with you. You hear me, boy?"

Christopher knew he would not be surprised. She had taught him well, so had Mr. Dexter. And he had learned on his own what it meant to be anything but white. It didn't matter what the one-armed Rebel said. It was expected. But change was on its way.

He stopped at the work shack where he and Mr. Dexter had spent so many hours together, Madie Marie too. He had finished the lettering on a piece of wood but had wanted to make it stand out, be special, maybe with flowers and birds. But all he had been able to do was carve out the letters M-AD-I-E M-A-R-I-E. One day, he thought, I'll finish it. He wanted everything to be perfect, her fancy coffin and her headstone, everything, before he left. He stood there, wondering if he should finish before he saw her and tell her he was leaving or if he should see her first and then finish.

When he arrived in her room, she opened her eyes immediately. No words were passed. He simply walked over to her bed and touched her arm, running his fingers down to her hand. And she softly held his fingers until all the strength and essence had left her body and her fingers relaxed.

He didn't know how long he stood there, thinking, realizing that his life was about to take a drastic change. There would be no Mr. Dexter or Madie Marie to create his life for him. Unless he succumbed to Chester and his stagnant and retrograde way of life, he would have to identify and build his own without Madie Marie or Mr. Dexter. It scared him.

He knew his first obligation, responsibility, above everything else, was to bury Madie Marie Princeton, the last of the Princeton family line. He couldn't claim to be a Princeton, had no right, although his life's essence was designed and promulgated by the Princeton legacy.

He would have to create his own name and a place to be and a life force strong enough to confront and survive what he suspected would be a turbulent tomorrow.

On the way back to the work shack, he encountered Chester again. He had not forgotten about him, but in his mind, he had relegated him to a position of insignificance. Chester, on the other hand, had in mind not only Christopher, but what his future would be with Princeton Manor.

"How is my cousin Madie Marie? I'm gonna nurse her back to good health. I know how to do that. Been in the Army. I know. That's where I lost this arm. I had to nurse myself some. Me and my cousin, we got big plans."

"She's dead."

"You know my grandpa told me when I found my cousin, I'd find my glory."

"Madie Marie Princeton is dead," Christopher repeated.

There was a long pause. Christopher started to walk away.

"Glory be!" Chester wailed. "My cousin, my only cousin."

"She's not your cousin. I told you that."

"Boy, you ain't got no right to tell me nothing. I tell you. Them men in the tavern told me all about you. Fancy pants."

"Anyway, I have things to do." He looked at Chester who stood in his path.

"I need her ready to be bury now. Put her in one of them boxes you got in that shed and put it in a hole, you know, grave. I got to start using the right words and all. I ain't down home with Grandpa no more. Ain't that something! Grave, that's the word! Okay, Chris?"

"My name is Christopher."

"Your name is whatever I tell you your name is. After you put her in that grave, I'll take it from there. My poor cousin! I'll need to pray over her, so she'll be sure to go to heaven. She was a good person, wasn't she? She was my cousin, so she had to be. My grandpa said we were all good people. That is why God is blessing me. You better get busy. And I don't care where the hole is. Up there in that plot is all right with me. After I do that burial thing, I will tend to your black ass."

Christopher was ignoring him. He had already created in his mind exactly how Madie Marie's burial would happen, exactly what he would do.

Of the three, he was the only one left. He decided he would put her next to Mr. Dexter. Maybe he would place her grave a little higher than Mr. Dexter, but not so high that people would wonder why she was placed higher than her husband. After all, he was the husband, the man. He thought about digging another grave for himself. But no one would ever put him there, not in the Princeton burial plot surrounded by a white picket fence.

"What's the matter? Hell, I done told you what I want to happen awhile back. Do I need to say everything again? I thought you was one of them smart niggers."

"You don't seem to understand," Christopher spoke softly, and his body reflected the sadness that had overcome him.

"You the one don't understand. You do what I say, you hear? This here is mines, all of it. A gift from God! Heck, if it wasn't for folks like my cousins and me, where would you be?"

"You got it all wrong. Where would you be without folks like me?" Christopher still spoke softly.

"You can't ask me no questions 'less I tell you you can. You ain't nothing till I tell you you something. That's the way it is. That's the way the Lord made it!"

"Then you don't mind if I leave." He turned his back to him and took a step in the opposite direction. But stopped suddenly and turned toward him.

"Whoa, you wait a minute, nigger! Don't want to kill you, not yet!" Chester jumped back, falling. He tried desperately to balance himself, but his only arm was on the opposite side. He struggled and fell to the ground.

"I must bury her!"

"Whoa, you . . . you wait right there till I get up! Help me here."

Clearly, if Christopher had wanted to attack him, he could easily have done so. But he simply stood and watched him struggle. And every time he took a step in Chester's direction, he struggled, falling backward again.

Christopher smiled and walked past him.

"You come back here! I ain't through with you! You hear me. That son of a bitch!"

When Chester finally caught up with Christopher, he had made it to the wood shack where he was surrounded by carving tools. He was preparing to finish that piece of wood that had Madie Marie's name on it and would be her headstone. Chester stopped at the door. They looked at each other.

"I know them Union soldiers are gonna be here real soon. I was planning on giving you a good beating before they got here. So, you would remember who is the master here. But..." And he looked at all the carving tools around Christopher and decided he best keep his distance.

"You remember they saved your ass this time. But you need to know. I ain't going nowhere. This here is my place. You don't know about all the fighting I been doing, do you? That's how I lost my arm fighting them niggers. Some nigger just shot it completely off. Had my gun in that hand too. They tell me I kept on killing niggers for a long time, even with one arm. That ought to tell you something about me, boy."

"You best be getting out of here and try to save that other arm," Christopher said calmly. "No telling what that army might do to you. Go! I just want to do right by her. The soldiers will be here by then. Don't think you want them to find you here."

"Guess ain't much I can do about them coming. When I get back here and you still around, I'm still gonna beat your ass. Grandpa, he didn't tell me nothing about this kind of stuff. But I know I'll be back. They ain't gonna stay here long. And you? You best be heading north or west, somewhere. I ain't never been to places like that myself. Don't know much about them, but they tell me white men in them places too. You remember that, boy!" And he was gone.

Christopher returned to his work, creating a masterpiece. It was far more beautiful than the one he had made for Mr. Dexter. And he looked upon it with pride and sadness and fear. She had been his face to the world. While the two of them had laughed when she told him how he used to hide under her dress, he realized he had spent his entire life under her dress, hiding.

He took the coffin, his most fancy one, and the well carved headstone to that plot of land Mr. Dexter had determined would be the Princeton family's final resting place. Then he brought her down and placed her in her coffin, closed the lid, and slid it into the freshly dug grave, slightly above Mr. Dexter. Thump, thump, thump. He heard each clump of soil as it covered her coffin.

When he was finished, he stood there looking at that empty spot that Mr. Dexter said was his. How long he stood there, he didn't know or care. Life was going to be different for him now. That's what he was thinking about. That empty spot, he knew, would always be empty.

He made his way back to his tree stump, looked around for a suitable piece of grass to chew on but found none. He took a seat on his tree stump, turning his head this way and that, thinking he heard horses coming. He waited.

(Lord, dear Load above, God Almighty, God of love,
please look down and see my people through.)

Walter

No one really knew much about Walter because he had lived a solitary life at old man Murphy's pigsty. When he took to sitting in the shade of a tree, any tree, and drawing pictures in the dirt and telling stories in what some called gibberish, everyone was surprised.

They knew he had been down there at the pigsty, but no one ever saw him. Why he went from that extreme state of solitude to becoming the storyteller everybody, young and old, was drawn to, was anybody's guess.

Slavery had just ended, and Old Man Murphy, owner of the plantation, had told his slaves to get off his property immediately. That, of course, was no problem. None of them had anything but what was on their backs, so leaving immediately was easy.

Some did refuse to leave; others scattered in various directions, all eventually heading north. There was another group who settled right off of Old Man Murphy's property line, down by the creek that ran right on the edge of his property. Walter was in this group. As a matter of fact, he could see what was once called the pigsty and that round boulder up on that hill where he had first seen Ann.

It was strange to see Walter laughing and enjoying himself with other people listening to his every word. Of course, some of the old-timers who had also been in slavery didn't find much of what he was saying funny or interesting. But some of them were there every day, listening and shaking their heads in disgust.

Invariably, one of them would say sometime like, "And what he got to bring up all that old slave stuff for? Need to just leave it be. It's done and over. Ain't no need to bring it up again. That's what I think."

Then there would be a series of, "Hmmm, ain't that the truth," or, "Lord have mercy. Why don't that old fool just hush up?" or, "Ain't nobody wanting to hear that old stuff, 'specially these young 'uns. They don't need to know 'bout that stuff anyway."

It wasn't clear why the old folk and the young ones showed up every time Walter stood and beckoned for all to join him under his personally picked shade tree, which was always near the creek. His stories were uniquely his, from his village in Africa to the pigsty.

Sometimes, he would stand and try to act out some salient points in his telling. As an old man, he was tall, better than six feet and always stood straight, stretching to his full height, sometimes with some effort. But, he was still muscular with intelligent and penetrating eyes that he often chose to close when telling his stories.

It was like he was painting every action, every detail on the inside of his eyelids. And his standing and acting out of various scenes and characters seemed to increase the excitement and mystery and drama of his stories.

The men where he was from in Africa had all been extremely tall, thin, and straight as arrows with long arms and legs, which hid the extraordinary strength under their brown or dark brown skin.

The most vivid scenes that seemed to be etched across his mind were the men standing tall and straight jumping up and down making strange high pitch sounds with their voices. They were happy and purposeful scenes.

He remembered that but not much else, except for the hand of the lady who walked next to him, not her face or her body, just her hand. He held that hand all the way from his village to that dreadful morning at the edge of the endless water.

His mother had been a captive of the tall people and lived with one of the elders as his slave. She had told him that he wouldn't grow to be as tall or thin as the men around him. But she was wrong. He did grow tall with that hidden strength.

When he was taken from his mother and the village, he wasn't surprised. He was a young man, approaching the time for the village manhood ritual, which wasn't available to him formally. But he had the heart of a warrior and when the time came for that ritual, he was there with the will and the desire to challenge, to participate. Heart pounding, strong, ready, waiting! But he also knew it was not for him.

He didn't know his age. No one cared anyway. He knew he would be taken away. It didn't matter that he had a warrior's heart. He was born of a slave mother he had left behind.

He couldn't remember how long they walked, but he did remember how much he enjoyed walking next to her, and snuggling next to her when the sun went down and the coolness of the evening covered their partially naked bodies.

And he remembered she held his hand all day and that regal bearing, that certain strength that was etched across her face and penetrating eyes passed through her hand to his. The curl of their fingers and tightness of their grip provided the passageway for her certain energy and strength to become his.

Then, one morning at the endless water's edge, some men came and took her away. He never saw her again. And as he looked around, he discovered all the females were gone, even the very young ones.

He was alone and that feeling of loneliness consumed and overwhelmed and angered and energized him. There was no one he wanted to talk to or be with. They all looked forlorn, desperate, and afraid. But he didn't.

She was gone, and he had to make whatever was about to happen to him tolerable and survivable. But he didn't know how to do that. All he knew or thought he knew was he had to be strong.

He and the other men were all put in chains and shackles and taken in small boats to the biggest boat he had ever seen. There, they were put down in a crowded, foul-smelling, dark hole. And the surrounding water pushed and shoved the boat at will, making it lurch and pitch, and roll and rock. All of that movement made some of them sick, and they threw up right there. And it stayed there, sliding here and there, over and under the other Africans who were close by. They couldn't move because they were chained together and secured to the wall and long boards.

He remembered how horrible it was with feces and pee, and vomit splashing against the walls and all over them. He remembered that, and the smell, the moans and piercing screams that got weaker and weaker until they were heard no more. There were men crying and groaning in languages he had never heard, but he understood their agony. And pink and red sores developed on some of the men as the filth ate into their once smooth skin.

Some men became gravely ill or died and were fed to the waiting, man-eating fishes. Other men became mystified and angry, and mad and crazed. They fought and lost. They too were thrown to the fishes. The Africans were always the losers, even though they were the majority onboard.

He had not gone through the ritual of manhood, that elaborate pageantry that every boy in his village had to pass through to become a man. There was joy at the end, a big, village-wide celebration that he could only enjoy from afar. Instead, another kind of manhood rite was quickly being thrust upon him. Different from what happened in his village and far more devastating. There was no celebration, no joy, no make-believe world. Onboard ship, there was only suffering.

Occasionally, there were trips topside to have buckets of salty water thrown on their bodies. He resented and resisted as much as he could. He was filthy and smelly, but there were no sores or scars on his body, except on his wrists and ankles where he had to often move quickly to avoid the diseased feces and other human waste splashing and running around his shackled body.

This, he concluded, was a journey into misery with no end in sight. And there were no opportunities or examples of strength or victory or jubilation, except for the woman who held his hand for all those miles. He would have to manufacture or imagine, minute by minute, hour by hour, day by day, his own survivable world, his own woman who would hold his hand.

But surviving the days and weeks and months of pee and feces and vomit, moans and groans, the stench, and his own hunger pangs that assaulted his very being were also the source of his inner strength.

There were days of calm and smooth sailing, but they were not enough to overcome the misery that was more often than not. The days were too long and the nights of darkness were even longer.

Then one day, he and others were brought to the deck to be washed down, greased all over, and prepared for what he discovered was the auction block. The months at sea had a tremendous impact on him and the others.

His anger and inner strength had grown. It grew more with his experience on the auction block with the humiliation of white hands trying to touch him as he fought them off. Then the auctioneer stepped forward and hit him as hard as he could on his shoulder, but he didn't budge.

"Look at this nigger here! This here is a good one, tall and strong. Hell, he can take a punch too." He looked at him and whispered, "Ain't nobody gonna buy you if 'n they can't touch you."

He didn't know what had been said and didn't care. He decided he would not look at the pale, stringy haired strangers whose hands wanted to touch, caress, and squeeze parts of his body.

He closed his eyes.

Then there was a voice, different from the others, more malleable.

"We'll take him," Paul Heller, the overseer for the Haynes Plantation, spoke up.

Most of the people in the crowd nodded their heads in smiling agreement that Haynes Plantation was indeed the place for this obstinate African.

On wobbly legs, salty sweat covering his body from the natural heat and his emotional turmoil, he and the others began their march to Haynes Plantation. He tried to look up at the clear-blue sky and around at the new vegetation but was slapped across the back with a huge strap. A man gestured for him to keep his head down and follow the man in front of him.

He did that.

But inside, that anger and strength and humiliation churned and solidified, giving him the courage and determination he knew he would need to not only survive but to overcome.

The Haynes Plantation had a reputation. Old man Murphy was known to punish his slaves frequently and cruelly. His reputation was known in all the proper circles, including on the slaves' grapevine. He was often referred to as the premiere slave breaker, a reputation and name that brought him immense joy and pride.

"A man that can't take care of his own niggers, hell, if he can't, he oughtn't have 'em. Send 'em to me! There will always be some dumb-ass nigger needing his ass kicked. My daddy taught me how to kick a nigger square in his ass. Ain't nothing to it." Those were the first words from his owner. He didn't understand them, but his expression made it quite clear it wasn't good.

He also said for every nigger he killed, he could buy two more to replace him, if he wanted. The old man was convinced that was the way the good Lord intended it to be or he wouldn't have the facility to always win and be an example for others. A slave was a slave, and that was all he or she was or could be, according to old man Murphy.

Old Man Murphy was known to have lots of opinions about slavery and was certain he could afford to have them. After all, "I'm a white man and a Christian. Course, I'm rich, got lots of land," he often said with a wide grin.

When Paul Keller, Old Man Murphy's overseer and the man with the malleable voice, bought this bunch of Africans from the auctioneer, he was certain they would be no problem. There was one, however, he did wonder about.

He was the young, strapping male who, for whatever reason, refused to be touched and wouldn't open his eyes. The old man hadn't seen this peculiar behavior before but assumed he would have no problems getting him straight with a good kick in the ass.

"Hold on there! What the hell is wrong with your eyes? Can't you see? How old are you? Shit, you don't know. You know your name? Don't you hear me talking to you? What, this nigger can't see or hear?" Old man Murphy's impatience began to show.

"Don't think he understands English. None of them do. Maybe we should take him back," Paul Heller spoke up quickly.

"Oh, they understand! Don't let them fool you."

He was partially right! There was this word that was used in reference to Africans. Nigger! He had heard it when he was in the hole of that ship, and now he hears it again on land. Over and over! But he thought it didn't sound right. It sounded hateful and evil and arbitrary. So, he would ignore it.

The old man had hired Paul because he saw him whip two men at the same time, white men who were known to be tough. He concluded he was just what was needed, a mean son of a bitch. Only to later find out he had been to some college where he was a boxer but thought he was intelligent and could reason with any man or slave.

"What? I ain't got time to be going back nowhere. Ain't gonna do it. If I have to, I'll pry that nigger's eyes open with my own hands. Get his ass in the wagon with the rest of 'em. We ain't got all day." Old man Murphy's frustration was directed at Paul and the slow progress they were making.

"Get 'em all up there. Ain't got time for no niggers to be walking," he laughed. "Riding might make them think they special or something."

The ride to the Murphy Plantation must have given the old man sufficient time to really think about this belligerent nigger not opening his eyes when he was told very clearly to do so. Maybe there was something wrong with him. He was young and kind of thin with long arms and looked like real good slave material. As far as he could see, there was no reason for him to have eye problems.

"Come on down off that wagon so I can get a damn good look at your eyes. Come on, ain't nobody gonna hurt you. Come on, now. Y'all help him a bit."

When he resisted help, the old man reached up and jerked him from the wagon to the ground. When he hit the ground, he didn't flinch. He remained there, facedown, almost motionless.

"Now get on up from there so we can talk. What they call you?" Old man Murphy stood over him with his hands on his hips. "Hell, you don't know what I'm saying. Shit, can't see either."

He remained prostrate on the ground.

"Let me talk to him," Paul Heller said as he moved closer, but the old man intervened.

"You ain't gonna say nothing that gonna make him act no different. This nigger don't understand English like you said! But I got something that he will understand. They always do!"

He then kicked him one time on his thigh. Still no response. He kicked him again, this time a little harder. The old man then kicked him three more times on the same thigh in the same spot, each time a little harder. Still no response.

"Let me try."

"You get on out of the way, Paul. Hell, been telling you all the time you ain't worth a penny when it comes to breaking these Africans. What you want me to call you, boy? I don't care what it is. Hell, it could be Bob or Bill or Harry or Hank! Got to call you something." Old man Murphy had been a plantation owner for years, so had his father. He thought he knew how to deal with any kind of slave who came his way. But this one was somehow different.

For some reason, when old man Murphy took a step toward him, he stood up, but his eyes still closed.

The old man was getting ready to stick his chest out until he realized how tall this African was. He backed up to the side of the road, some ten yards away, and stood on a little embankment, hoping that would give him some height.

"Just don't stand there like a knot on a log. Look at you! Get over here. You better open your eyes so you can see what your master looks like before and after he kicks your ass. What the hell wrong with you, boy? I paid good money for your dumb ass! And your name is Sam. Can you remember that? You better. Dumb son of a bitch!"

It took at least a year of the old man's beatings, tying him naked to a tree for the ants to crawl all over him during the day and the mosquitoes to roam and buzz, and bite him at night. Even threatening, with knife in hand, to cut off one ear and two fingers didn't motivate him to open his eyes.

One day, the sun was high and the air was still and the moans and groans of the field slaves could be heard far and wide. It must have been the hottest day of the year. The old man, sweat pouring down his hairless chest, took a green leaf and tickled Sam's genitals. When the blood rushed through his body, the old man, with knife in hand, grabbed his genitals. Sam suddenly opened his eyes and looked at old man Murphy who dropped the knife and took two steps away from him, stumbling but never taking his eyes away.

It was what he saw that caused him to react as he did. There was no anger or fear, but there was a fierce and penetrating intensity. Old man Murphy had never seen that in a slave's eyes. Slaves didn't look into their master's eyes. But he did.

The old man's anger increased, and his determination to break him multiplied. He had lost this battle, but he was the master and he, old man Murphy, never ever lost. He only had to find another way to break him and make him his kind of nigger.

He decided to isolate him, make him spend his days standing in the sun in a spot where the grass had turned a perpetual brown. No one was to talk to him or look his way. His nights were spent in a little bug inflicted toolshed, no bed, no place to lay down, tools everywhere. Yet every morning when he came out to meet the sun, he was standing tall.

Old Man Murphy thought that isolating and ignoring him would bring him around. But other slaves seeing him just standing around thought they should be able to do the same. Not only that, but word was getting around to the other slave owners that Old Man Murphy had finally met his match. His reputation as a badass had been sufficiently challenged.

"So, what the hell am I gonna do with you, Sam? I suppose I could just kill your black ass. I could do that as easy as taking my next step. You see that, don't you, Sam? I've gotten something out of every nigger on my place. But you? Nothing but shit and piss from my feeding your African ass."

He could feel Sam looking down on him. "Don't be looking at me. You know better. Lift your shirt up there, let me see if there's any more room on your back for a scar or two. Now how did I know you wasn't gonna do that? Get your ass over there!"

Old Man Murphy and Paul grabbed him. Sam shook them both off and stretched to his full height.

"Look how tall this nigger is," Old Man Murphy said. "Guess you think you a man, huh? Look at him. This boy would be a good breeder, huh?"

Paul didn't respond right away. They both just looked at Sam, marveling at his height.

"Well, he would, but..."

"Ain't no but, Paul. Why is it always a but with you? Either he will or he won't. And ain't no won't for a nigger. Just 'cause you can read real good, been to school and all, you don't know what I know. You haven't been out here with these niggers like I have. Why I got you as my overseer I don't know."

"If I weren't here, you probably would have beaten or killed most of your slaves and no telling who else. Your father knew what he was doing when he told you to hire me."

"Well, he's dead and gone now and ain't telling nobody nothing. So, just hush up, Paul, I need to think here."

Old man Murphy finally decided what he would do with Sam. He would take him to the pigsty. Maybe he will run away and the old man can hunt him down and shoot him.

"He'll be gone in a week," Paul agreed and spoke with certainty.

"Let him try." The old man was just as certain, even though the pigsty was several miles from the big house and Sam would be there by himself.

"What? Because he's afraid of you? I don't think so." Paul was waving his hand, indicating his certainty that Sam wasn't afraid of the old man.

"Nah, that nigger ain't got sense enough to be scared." Old man Murphy's response was deliberate and thoughtful, and his expression confirmed his certainty.

"Or too much sense," Paul laughed.

"Don't be laughing. If he ran off, I win. 'Cause then we will find his ass and I would let you have the honor of killing him."

"You best be careful," Paul cautioned. "His is mental. Yours is physical. Don't think that's enough."

"What you talking about? Watch!" Old man Murphy snapped. "He can't live down there with them stinky pigs, smelling their slop and shit, that will drive him right to me. Watch."

"Think so, huh? What if he stays a week or so? You free him?"

"Hell no! I didn't say that. You know how filthy them pigs are. He will have to walk around that pigsty barefooted. Shit, he won't last a week. Mark my word!"

"But if he does?"

"Nothing! Enough. I've heard enough. I don't know what else you could say."

Neither of them realized being isolated was exactly what he wanted. Somewhere during his travel as a slave, he had resolved to never bring another human being into this horrible world of misery.

The first time the old man and Paul traveled down to the pigsty, Old Man Murphy had actually stopped before crossing the creek. His grandfather had named it

Murphy's Creek, at least the part that ran across his land and included the pigsty.

And there he was old man Murphy's Sam, standing in the creek washing his feet. And on the bank of the creek were buckets and jars and a large pot all filled with water. The old man was shocked. Paul, who had walked several feet ahead of him, turned and looked at him.

"What is he doing, Paul?"

"Well, it looks like he's collected water, and now he's washing his feet," Paul was smiling. "I can see that much, Paul."

He saw them. He didn't wave or beckon them to come. He just looked at them and continued to wash his feet.

The old man turned and started back toward the big house. Paul followed, looking back occasionally, but wondering what was on the old man's mind.

The second time, they actually made it across the creek and to the pigsty. He was nowhere to be found. He had moved the pigs to the other side of the shack so they would be in more shade. He had dug up a wallowing pool so they would not have to wallow in their own shit and slop every day. He had also built two fences that allowed them to go out to a green area where he had planned to make a garden just for them to root and dig. The place was as clean as any one person could make it, considering how pigs live.

The old man was speechless for a while but then smiled.

"See, I told you he would run off."

"Why would he do all this and leave?" Paul questioned. "Just to show me. Niggers can be that way sometimes."

"Show you what? What way?" Paul was feeling pretty good. He had been right about Sam and began looking around for him.

"This, all of this! And I win. He's gone. When my men bring his ass back here, I'm going to dump his ass in a pile of pig-shit and make him stay there for a day or two. And then, I'll let you kill his ass. I'm tired of messing with him."

"And where are you getting the pigsty with all of that pig shit? Not here! There's no pig shit anywhere that I can see.

"He did a good job."

"Oh, hush up, Paul."

They both turned when they heard someone whistling. It was him. He saw them but ignored them.

"Sam, Sam!" The old man's face turned red as he called Sam again and again, and he ignored him and kept walking toward the shack. Looking puzzled, Paul walked toward him. He stopped immediately, stood with his head cocked and looked at him and then at the old man as if they were strangers.

"See, he is fine. The pigsty is fine. Perhaps we should go now." Paul was anxious, fearing the old man might try to fulfill his plan and try to capture him. Paul knew it would take more than the two of them.

"I ain't going nowhere. I ain't told this nigger to do none of this shit. Who told him? You?"

"I didn't tell him anything," Paul answered. "I think we should go, sir."

"Told you! I ain't going nowhere." And with that, the old man pulled out his pistol. "When I call you this time, you better get on your knees and start praying to your God to save your black ass. Shit, I don't know if you got a God."

"Whatever you got, you best pray to him."
"Whoa, sir!"
"Ain't no whoa now! I done took all I can bear from this nigger."
"What? All he did was fix this place up."
"I ain't told him to do that. Who told him to build that cabin?"
"Sam, Sam, Sam!" Paul waved to him.

Still, there was no response or move. He continued to look at the old man who cocked his pistol.

"Sam, Sam, Sam!" Paul became frantic, looking back and forth. He feared the old man might actually shoot him this time.

Still, he didn't move or change his expression. In his mind, he was hoping that the next move from the old man would be to pull the trigger. Then it would be over. He had spent his time and the loneliness was trying to get his attention. But if the old man pulled the trigger, he would no longer need to think about anything. It would be all over. So, he waited and waited and nothing happened.

The old man had turned and walked away toward the creek. Paul followed with a smile on his face, greatly relieved. Old man Murphy never returned. Paul did. As a matter of fact, he returned many times, and he and Sam would throw pebbles into the creek and watch the sun disappear into the earth. Paul did all the talking. And the man Paul knew as Sam never said a word. That had always been his way, not to talk.

But when Sam saw her for the first time and they established eye contact, no matter the distance, a powerful connection was made. And with that distant eye contact, he suspected he had told her more than any words in whatever language could ever say.

He didn't like or want to feel or think that his desire for her had overpowered his resolve to remain free of any human contact or involvement, especially with a woman.

She had been standing by that big boulder, the one that was perfectly round on top, where the sun would flash its brilliance and sometimes caress with its power to create colors and warmth. It was the one that stood on that little hill all by itself not far from his newly built cabin.

She just stood there for several moments, and then she was gone. It was like she wanted him to see her. Each day for about a week, she would appear, standing next to that boulder that sparkled in the sun, especially when she was standing next to it.

Then one day, she had two older Indians with her, a man and a woman. They watched him for a long time as he took care of his daily chores. Then they were gone, but she remained.

He decided, trying to fight the urge but ultimately giving in, that the next time he saw her, he would go to her. And he did. She stood there, and he slowly walked toward her. The closer he got, the more beautiful she became. He had never seen an Indian woman before, and the sun on her reddish-tan skin and the black braid that ran down her back made him stop. He wanted to turn around, because he knew he was about to go against his promise, against his will. That's why the pigsty was a perfect place for him. He never thought he would encounter anyone like her.

He stood there next to her, neither one of them said anything. They just looked out across the vast stretch of land.

She touched his arm and said, "Annie." And he touched her and said, "Walter."

Then she was gone. It was that touch that confirmed his irretrievable position.

He stood there after she left, shaking his head, trying to refocus his mind. And it struck him that he had just named himself Walter. He smiled and thought he would be Walter from then on. He even said it aloud several times. "Walter! Walter!" He knew that was his first debilitating step, but he didn't seem to have the will to stop.

The next time he saw her several days later, he started walking toward her, and she met him halfway. He noticed she had a bag with her. They smiled at each other. She followed him down the little hill and into his one-room cabin. And she stayed.

Not one word was passed between them. They seemed to know each other, like they had been together for years, maybe hundreds of years. That contact, that ability to look into each other's eyes and know was the second step. He knew there was no turning back.

When Paul came to visit, he was astonished to find her there and even more confounded when Sam pointed at her and said, "Annie," and at himself and said, "Walter."

Then one morning, months later, Walter woke up, and she was gone. Walter, and he thought of himself as Walter, instinctively knew he would miss her but thought that maybe his promise to himself, his will, wasn't lost. But each morning, he would look up at that boulder, empty of her presence.

The next time he saw her, she was standing in the cabin doorway with a baby in her arms. He was glad to see her. She looked at him and then at the baby several times. And he knew. His promise had been broken.

But she smiled and tried to put the baby in his arms. He stood stiff-like, backing away. He left her standing there, holding the baby in her outstretched arms. He walked down to the creek. She followed and stood behind him. He had done the unthinkable. He had brought another being into a world of misery.

Several days later, when Paul came to visit for what turned out to be his last time, he had smiled as usual, but this time it was a bigger smile. He had great news. He told Walter there was a war going on between the North and the South, but because Walter was so isolated, he thought he would escape any involvement and the fighting wouldn't, most likely, come his way. When Annie and the baby came out of the cabin to join them, he paused for a long time.

They walked to the creek and sat on big stones, and she, holding the baby, sat on the ground at Walter's feet. Paul told them that President Abraham Lincoln had signed a paper called the Emancipation Proclamation. He was free.

Paul was elated, and with tears in his eyes, he said it again. "Walter, you're free."

Walter stood and started toward his cabin. Annie and her baby followed. But he stopped and looked at Paul whose tears freely ran down his face.

"You're free, Walter, a free man."

Walter turned and started toward his cabin. Annie and their baby followed.

(Something within me that banishes pain;
Something within me I can't explain, all
that I know there is something within.)

Walter's Line

On this particular Monday morning, Etta Jean had decided the time had come. And as she looked up at the sun, she said it aloud: "This is my last day on this earth. Walter, your wish will come true today."

It was as if the sun had agreed and decided to inflict and center its smothering and penetrating heat on the top of her head, causing the sweat to pour from her thin and frail body and her thick coarse hair to roll up in unruly knots. At the same time, a chill exploded in her core and fought with the heat for supremacy.

That was the change that really got her attention, the explosions that caused her to chill and have bouts of fever in alternating bursts. And at the same time, causing her thick black hair to drip and sparkle with perspiration and her skinny arms and legs to quiver and shake. There was nothing left, nothing for her to do, nothing for her to protect.

Of course, she often thought her time had come, especially during the summer and on Sundays. But this time was different. That explosion in her core caused her to quickly search for newspaper, old rags, anything, and run from her table, as quickly as she could, to the outhouse. Not once, but several times! And one time, she didn't quite make it. That, not making it, was another sign that the day had finally come.

There would be no messing around this time, she decided, as she murmured a soft and weak, "Thank you, Jesus." She had paused and turned to look at the old outhouse, thinking this would be her last trip. No more rubbing together of newspaper to make it soft or having to hold her breath to deal with somebody else's stench.

This had to be the day! Why else would she feel and think with such certainty that the end was near? Walter was gone. Willie Lee was gone. And she could hardly make it back from the outhouse to her waiting table and foot pan of salty water.

Often on these Mondays when she would think the day had finally arrived, she would stretch out on her bed buck naked, hoping she would leave this world the way she came in. But often her imagination got the best of her and she would think about some man, any man, coming in, finding her, and not be able to resist having his way with her. She would fight, of course, knowing she would lose.

Sometimes, she would go to sleep thinking about that and wake up disappointed. Not only because she did indeed wake up, but also to find herself on her stomach with her right hand with its long, hard fingers in her thick black pubic hair.

Etta Jean didn't know much about her birth and no one told her much about her family. And she didn't seem to remember much about whatever she had been told. She was born up by the pigsty and her mother was an Indian woman named Annie. That was it.

Sadie was an old ex-slave who had been on Old Man Murphy's plantation all of her life, born and raised there. When the old man told all his slaves they had to be gone from his place by the next morning because slavery was over, Sadie was one of them who left but didn't go very far. She and a bunch of other ex-slaves formed a community on the north side of the creek not far from the pigsty and Murphy Plantation property line.

It wasn't unusual for slaves to build communities close to their old plantation. Some didn't know what else to do or where to go. They stayed close by, while some of the other slaves were braver and struck out for parts unknown, usually going north. But one old timer told old man Murphy he didn't know anything about freedom and he was staying right where he was. He wasn't the only one that felt this way.

Old Sadie, no one knew if she was old or not, was the person the Indian woman, Annie, had walked up to, put a cute little baby in her arms, pointed at it and said "Etta Jean," left, never to return.

She, Etta Jean, was brought up around a bunch of ex-slave women but always within the eyesight of Old Sadie. She didn't belong to anyone in particular. She was here and there, eating and sleeping whenever and wherever she could but never too far from Sadie.

She was the one that taught Etta Jean to put her feet in a pan of cold salty water every morning. It would make her feel better. Start her day off just right. Etta Jean didn't know if it did or not. She just automatically got that old beat-up pan every morning, added salt and water, and put her long skinny feet in it.

She could have or should have grown up to be a beautiful woman, desired by many men. But there was something inside of her that kept that beauty from emerging. She had thick black hair. Some folk would call it African and Indian hair. Her features were keener than most, which meant she didn't have a big, wide nose or thick lips. She had been a fine-looking baby. But after a few years, the beauty that should have developed simply didn't. It was there, at least, the old women thought it was, but somehow, it refused to come out. It seemed to have been concealed deep inside and found no reason to reveal itself.

Etta Jean was Walter's daughter, but she didn't know that until Sadie told her she thought that's who her father was. Etta Jean had never seen him or didn't remember seeing him.

That's why when this man called Walter started hanging around the community, she wasn't particularly curious. He was just another ex-slave who chose to stop at their community, beside he always had this young boy with him, his son, she assumed.

Then one day, when Sadie and she were walking to the creek for water, she came face to face with Walter. They looked at each other and she felt a jolt that at first frightened her, causing her to drop her head and freeze. Finally, after she looked at him, he was still looking at her. Then he smiled, nodding his head. She remembered smiling back and feeling nervous and excited but afraid.

She saw him several more times, and each time, she felt a stronger connection to him. He would always smile and nod. Etta Jean wondered why.

And then he took to sitting in the shade of a tree, any tree, and drawing pictures in the dirt and telling stories about his life at the pigsty in what the old-timers called gibberish. He would have all the children laughing, not that the stories were really funny, but it was the way he told them. And when he talked about pigs, that made everybody laugh, even the old folks.

And sometimes, he would dance like the men did in his African village. It was clear he enjoyed jumping up and down, dancing. Sometimes, this little boy would get in his way, and he would push him in Etta Jean's direction.

There was something magnetic about Walter, and regal. A powerful energy exuded from his body, especially his eyes. He had smooth, dark brown skin, except for the scars that covered his back, which were dark, shiny, puffy lines with white and pink specks here and there.

There was something that made her feel like Walter was sending her and only her a special message in a language more powerful than any she had ever heard or felt. It was like a piercing call, cry out for help, even if he was smiling.

And it seemed far too powerful for her to ignore. And the young boy, who couldn't have been much younger than she, started standing around her, close enough for her to notice, which she found strange, except sometimes, he looked like Walter and sometimes he didn't.

It was all a mystery to her until Walter told that story about the slave who was nameless until he met an Indian woman and had two children by her. It wasn't like his other stories, and when he told it or part of it that one time, only one time, he stood tall and still and regal, eyes opened wide, looking directly at Etta Jean. It was like a powerful energy consumed his body, and its only release was telling this particular story.

There was no laughter, not from him or Etta Jean. The others, the younger ones in the crowd, did smile every now and then. And the older people stood still, like they knew. They understood a special moment, a huge moment, was upon them. They listened quietly. But he looked at Etta Jean with such intensity that it made her nervous. She wanted to shy away, but it was far too powerful for her to ignore.

And the older people understood and appreciated that they were witnessing a special moment, a huge moment. They listened quietly.

She felt like every word he said enter her body and become a part of her being, especially when he talked about wanting his seed to be the last of his line. The suffering and the misery, and the dehumanizing would end with him. She not only heard those words but felt them.

He stood there for a moment, shaking his head, and breathing harder than usual. And he looked off into the distance and looked at her. Twice he did this, looked off into the distance, and then at her. Then, he walked off, and she followed. How far and how long they walked, she had no idea. When he stopped, he was standing next to a huge, smooth, round boulder. He placed his hand on the boulder and told her his story.

She was a beautiful Indian woman with long, thick black braids. And that day when she stood next to him, touched his arm and said, "Annie," that's when he knew it was going to happen. She was going to end his promise to be the last of his seed.

Confirmation was quick. He had only to touch his chest. And out of the blue, without any thought, he said, "Walter." He had no idea where that name came from. It just flashed across his mind. He wasn't sure where or if he had heard it before. Walter! It stayed there floating around in his head as if that's where it was supposed to be. Walter, that's the name he would go by.

They stayed in his little cabin for a long time, months, maybe a year. Time was of no consequence. They spent their days working around the pigsty, taking time off to walk slowly in the creek. And at night, they would look at the stars and moon and he would enter her.

But then, she disappeared. He woke up one morning, and she was gone. He didn't know what to think, so he didn't think anything.

But he would look up at the big boulder every now and then to see if she were there, sometimes two, three times a day. He had all these mixed feeling. One moment, he was happy she was gone, so he could return to his solitary chosen life. The next moment, he was missing her and their walks in the creek each day. He didn't know what to do, so he did nothing.

Then he stopped talking, took a deep breath, and looked up at the sky. He removed his hand from the boulder and started walking back toward the community. Etta Jean didn't know what to do. So, she followed him.

The next day when Walter took his seat under the shade tree and beckoned to others to join him so he could continue to tell his stories, most of the young ex-slaves didn't return. Only the old folks did, and of course, Etta Jean.

Even the little boy had disappeared. But Walter continued. This time, he stretched his long legs out, which revealed the white crust and thickness that covered the bottom of his worn, shoeless feet. He looked at Etta Jean with the same level of intensity as before. He closed his eyes and spoke.

"Over time, I thought less and less about her, thinking it was the best thing to do. If she stayed away, nothing would happen, and I could keep my promise. I reminded myself, and I often had to, that I had told myself many times that I would never bring another person into such a miserable life. I meant that! Slavery was not life. It was drudgery and the stealing of minds and souls. And with her gone, my success was assured. Yet I still sometimes looked up at the boulder." Walter never did finish that story, never said anything about Etta Jean or the little boy. No one was interested or listening, except Etta Jean. It made her angry, because she wanted to hear the entire story.

She knew about Annie, because Sadie had mentioned her and she was in his story. The old women ex-slaves enjoyed telling their stories about the strange Indian woman with long black braids putting a baby in Sadie's arms. And each story had its personal nuance, reflecting the character of the teller and filled with those personal knowings that informed their differences.

Walter later continued to tell other stories, but he never finished the one Etta Jean was most interested in, the one about the slave and Annie, the Indian woman.

She learned a lot from the old women in the community, and that learning set a particular course for her. And Sadie was the most influential. She taught Etta Jean to pick up white folks' dirty clothes and wash, iron, and deliver them, all to be done in a specific time frame. She learned that all she needed to wear was a roomy dress and sometimes shoes, because no one cared how she looked. She learned the next day would be the same as the previous day. That's what slavery was like. But slavery was over.

But it was Walter who made her look inside. Her father who never said, "I am your father." He told stories to all who would listen. He was the community's storyteller.

But there was that particular story and the penetrating look he gave Etta Jean that seemed to connect the two of them in an ironclad clasp.

She thought he was the most handsome man she had ever seen, even though his hair was grey and matted and his toothless smile was usually with a closed mouth. The scars on his back and legs, which he didn't try to hide, were not marks of ritual or pride. It seemed like he wanted his audience to see them. Often, he made them part of his stories. They were part of his terrifying reality, one that he didn't want anyone from his seed to experience.

Etta Jean learned a lot from him and consequently understood why he wanted his line to end. She knew that what he saw and what she had to do day after day after slavery was over wasn't much better than slavery itself.

The biggest and most important thing to Walter was the opportunity he had to tell his stories. It was clear that he relished telling his personal story, not just the one about the slave and Annie, but the funny things pigs did, and how he used to talk to them. And then, there were other stories he told in a very different manner and tone, like the one about the woman whose hand he held on their march to the shore of the endless water and the auction and old man Murphy and his plantation.

But the boy who followed him around each day? Walter never mentioned him. There were no stories about him or for him, even on the day Walter closed his eyes forever. He told none and left none.

What Walter said on that day to Etta Jean confused her, even when she thought about it later. Maybe, she often thought, she had not heard him clearly. She remembered his saying something about seeing inward sometimes interfering with seeing outward. Then he told her, and she heard this very clearly, that the boy who followed him around was her mother's son, her brother. She had died trying to give birth to two babies. Willie was the only one to come out. And Walter, he never said he was their father. She remembered he had frowned. He died that day with that frown on his face. Etta Jean felt it. She knew, she decided he knew, his burden had been passed on.

Etta Jean called her brother, Willie Lee. He would grow to be tall like Walter, his father, and handsome and obviously smart, traits that didn't impress her. He also had the same features as Walter. He (stood like him, too. And when he would say certain words, his intonation sounded like Walter.

Some folk say Walter died because he didn't want to see Etta Jean or Willie Lee grow up free of slavery but not free of the life slavery left behind.

Etta Jean was older than Willie Lee. She knew that Walter, without ever saying so, would expect her to show him the way.

Willie Lee grew up to be known, at least by the white folk, as a nice colored boy who sometimes worked at the general store and the various moonshine operations scattered here and there across the countryside. He lived with Etta Jean but slept in the back of the general store or at the moonshine site.

He was known to make some white ladies nervous or uncomfortable, because they thought he looked at them too long. Of course, there were others who didn't object to his looking because they did the same to him. Some of the white men thought he needed to be watched or taken out in the woods and taught a fatal lesson.

But Willie Lee was spared because the white folks with money had plans for him. The local white dentist, Dr. Whitaker Ramsey, and a few other wealthy white citizens got together and pooled enough money to send Willie up north to dentistry school.

One of the white ladies Etta Jean ironed for told her that Dr. Ramsey was tired of putting his fingers in niggers' mouths. He was willing to pay for Willie Lee to learn how it was done. So, he could be spared the humiliation, although she suspected there were other places the good dentist stuck his fingers that he didn't find humiliating.

Thus, Etta Jean's brother, Willie Lee, went off to dentistry school somewhere up north. Of course, this never did sit well with Etta Jean. No one ever offered to send her to school anywhere. What she was offered was the opportunity to iron white folks' clothes. That was it.

With Willie Lee gone, she was alone, not that he was ever there. He never did come around much after those incidents in the woods. What really made her mad was his allowing them to happen, just standing there and not stopping them. What she didn't understand was how often she thought about each time. She could be in the outhouse, holding her nose, and it would cross her mind. Sometimes in vivid details, especially the first time it happened. Walter would have never allowed that to happened. But Willie Lee, he just stood there!

She never told anyone what Willie Lee had done. There was no one to tell. Walter was gone. She didn't see much of Willie Lee. But she remembered how he and his white buddies had chased her into the woods. They, his friends, tore her dress off, looked at her skinny body, and felt between her legs and made her hurt. And then, they laughed. And Willie Lee just stood there.

That was the first time, and she remembered hurting for days. She stopped talking to Willie Lee after that, and when she looked at him, he would always shy away.

The second time, they really had their way with her. All four of them. She knew she was being raped, because she felt them inside her. It hurt for a long while.

She had fought until she couldn't fight anymore. Then, she just closed her eyes and let it happen. But she didn't cry; regardless of the pain, she refused to cry. And Willie Lee, he just stood there.

The third time she bit her lip, but it was different. She just looked at Willie Lee who just stood there. She wasn't sure, but somewhere in the midst of their raping her, she thought she may have enjoyed it. But what troubled her most was Willie Lee. What they did to her wasn't new to black girls. She had heard about white boys and men catching black gals in the woods and raping them. All the time! More than people knew! It was like nobody cared.

And what Willie Lee did, just standing there watching them rape his sister, that's what bothered her. She was still confused. Was it what they did to her or what Willie Lee allowed them to do? Maybe it would have happened anyway, regardless of what Willie Lee didn't do. She was, after all, a black gal!

Sometimes at night in her bed with her hand between her legs, she would wonder if it had happened again, if Willie Lee would have told them to stop, that she was his sister. She knew he wouldn't have. But in retrospect she wondered if she really wanted him to stop them. She thought about it often because it was the first and the last time anyone ever touched her.

There were nights when she would run her hands over her body and feel its vacantness and her small insignificant breast and her skinny thighs and realized she wouldn't even have the opportunity to have a white man's baby. No one desired her or was desperate enough to come inside her shack. She didn't feel rejected or shunned. This, she concluded, had to be part of Walter's plan, his preordained plan.

Dr. Ramsey died a few years after Willie Lee's return from his success at the dentistry school. And the speculations on the cause of his death were from as simple as he died of old age, although he was not that old, to his wife finding out about him and his nurse, not to mention his enormous appetite for nigger gals. But because Mrs. Ramsey's brother was the sheriff, those possibilities were never looked into.

The best explanation or rumor, which made some people nod their heads in agreement and others shout foul and want revenge and still others to laugh to the point of tears, was that the spit or saliva from those colored patients' mouths had finally caught up with him and poisoned him to die. Nigger spit did this, they said.

Dr. Ramsey's death left Willie Lee as the only dentist in town, which, of course, caused some problems. Either white folks had to go to Willie Lee for their dental needs or travel ten miles or further to the next town to find a white dentist. Some white folk didn't mind Willie Lee prodding around in their mouths. Folks like him cooked for them, took care of their babies (sometimes giving them tit), washed and ironed all their clothes (including their spotted underwear), and performed other personal and intimate chores. Some white ladies wanted it all, the cooking, cleaning, and ironing, and welcomed Willie Lee's fingers prodding around in their mouths, and Etta Jean suspected other places too.

She always knew that Willie Lee liked white women. He and his white buddies would chase white girls and black gals into the woods, just like they did her, and Willie Lee would be smiling and smelling like white girls for days.

But there were white men who couldn't afford to take a day off to get their wives or daughters or mothers to the next town for dental care. These were the men who either had to listen to their wives complain about their need for dental work or control their imagination when their wives or daughters or mothers went into Willie Lee's office and he closed the door behind them.

"Willie Lee, can you do this? Willie Lee, can you do that?" It was like he was still the delivery boy in the general store and doing handy work for the moonshine customers. They concluded his being a dentist was no reason for him to be uppity and not do what they told him to do. One old white man told him just because he went to school up north and became a dentist didn't mean anything had really changed. He simply didn't work for the general store and the moonshiners anymore.

All the things he had learned in school and the fact he wore a suit with a watch chain in his vest pocket every day didn't impress these white folks at all. And it didn't impress Etta Jean either, which he seemed to realize, not that he cared.

Dr. Ramsey, the white dentist, had only associated with folks at his social level. For Willie Lee, the dentist, that was problematic, since all the coloreds worked as laborers or domestic workers, if they were fortunate to work at all. He had to become more of a loner, choosing not to associate too often with Etta Jean or the few coloreds he grew up with. They, after all, were not at his social level.

Etta Jean didn't care much for Willie Lee before he left for dentist school and cared even less when he returned. She always thought of him as not Walter-like enough, not understanding Walter's wish, and maybe not nothing it.

There were several other reasons she didn't care for him. The main one, the one that really got her attention, was his showing up at exactly the same time her mother disappeared. She knew what Walter said, but that wasn't enough. Even when he told her there had been two babies inside her belly, but Willie Lee was the only one to come out. The other one refused and stayed inside, protected from the cruel world of those who wanted to perpetuate the slave culture. When it died inside Etta Jean's mother's belly, it took her with it.

Willie Lee had denied Etta Jean her mother's love, wisdom, and understanding. She never got to know what she looked like, the color of her eyes, how she would have hugged her and smiled at her and spanked her bottom. And whether she had a long black braid like they say.

Walter didn't have a drinking problem. Of course, Willie had his first drink when he started working at the store and never stopped. He had spent his years running errands from the whiskey still to the general store for the moonshiners. Of course, one of the moonshiners and the owner of the general store were the same person. Willie Lee's drinking was well known, at least among the white folk. Often his pay had been in moonshine whiskey.

Etta Jean knew and some of the other colored folks knew about his drinking. They were glad to see him go off to school, hoping he would get away from the drinking and the low life he was forced to live. The colored community wanted him to return home in triumph, their hero, an example of a smart colored man defying all odds. They wanted him to be that shining beacon of hope. But Etta Jean had hoped that Walter's spirit had stretched itself across time and space and became embedded in Willie Lee.

He did well pulling colored folks' teeth but died rather suddenly, several years after returning home. They say he was sitting in his dentist chair with his bloody white coat on when they found him. And the blood the sheriff found on the floor? Well, he said it was probably that of Willie's last patient. Some colored folk said the blood around his chair was really red, like white folk blood, and that intermingling dripping dark blood, which the sheriff never mentioned, was probably Willie's.

Walter's line would end with Etta Jean. Willie Lee would not carry it any further. It made Etta Jean really happy, much happier than she thought she could ever be.

She didn't go to Willie Lee's burial that morning. She said it was too hot with the sun beaming down on her head and that strange inner chill that worked together to make her sure, certain, that the time had come. With those final acts, Willie Lee's burial and those explosions that wrecked her body, it was time to put the Walter's line to rest.

As she slowly moved her spoon around in her bowl of cold, lumpy grits, she realized she had nothing to look forward to or think about or protect now. The only thing left was the ironing of Mrs. Bickford's clothes.

What would she think about now, pushing her grits away with a frown on her face? She then, seemingly without thought, took her soaking long and bony feet out of the pail of cold, salty water and rubbed them gently. Her long thin arms and spindly legs seemed to be too long for her short and narrow torso. She gently stroked the inside of her thighs, pausing as if in thought, perhaps concluding that the temptation to move her fingers just a bit higher for the last time would avail absolutely nothing. Never did. She smiled in triumph as she started on her final trip into her little shack.

Etta Jean never did do the Bickford's ironing. On that day, all she wanted to do was honor Walter and end it, just let it be.

(Soon we'll be done with the troubles of this world. No more weeping and a wailing.)

Without Redemption

Lefty and Harlan had been traveling for weeks, actually several months. Their first mistake was to buy passage on a freighter going south to the Islands, rather than North and then East to Liverpool, England, then on to Spain. Neither one of them was worried at first because as Lefty explained, it was an opportunity to look at the slave trade business first hand. Harlan, however, wasn't really interested in slavery. As far as he was concerned they had enough gold, which they had hidden in a little cave they had discovered right near Rich Mountain, to do whatever they wanted. Nor would Harlan agree to exchange their gold for Confederate or Union paper money. Instead, they agreed to hide their gold in that very remote cave that they both concluded would be safe. For Harlan investing his gold in the profitable slave trade business wasn't going to help him find the kind of wife he wanted, even though it probably would make him richer. He decided he would take a break from the pursuit for gold and find himself that perfect wife. He had been told that the prettiest, and consequently the most perfect women in the world, came from this special little village in Spain, just a few miles from the central Spanish Portugal border. And that's where they were headed. Lefty agreed, reluctantly, to go with him. Why? He wasn't sure. He could have taken his share of the gold and brought a plantation and some slaves or a tavern with a few working white and nigger gals. But he didn't. Maybe he was influenced by Harlan's strange ability to find more ways to discover gold and use that gold to make more gold. Lefty had agreed that Harlan would have the responsibility for hiding the bags of gold, as long as he knew where he could find them. That had been a safe arrangement, reflecting their different view of the place of gold in their life.

"You know what, Lefty? Gold can do almost anything, except find the perfect wife. It can be of some help for sure, but I don't know if that's enough. Oh, you can find a woman who like gold, that's easy. But finding the perfect one? Well, that's more tough." Smiling

Lefty laughed out loud. "Ain't no such thing as a perfect wife, Harlan. Remember that black gal I had? Remember?" Lefty shook his head from side to side. "Well, you can shake your head all you want, but you remember. You wanted some of her stuff. You could of gotten some too. I didn't care. Somebody was always getting some when I wasn't around."

Grinning. "I didn't want none of that gal. And she was pretty, too." It was clearly written all over Harlan's face. He was not telling the truth.

"That gal? Now she was good at whatever she decided to do with her stuff. Getting in and out was more than just getting in and out. But you know what, Harlan?" Laughing. "Even with stuff like that, she wasn't perfect. She would of had to be white to be perfect, I guess. Course, I ain't never had no white girl, so I don't know what make them perfect, except they're white.

"You would think as old as I am I would of had me some white stuff by now. Hell, I could have bought me some, huh? When I was a little kid I used to play around with this girl, and she was blond, too, lived right up the hill from my mama's house, but I never done it to her, never tried, and looking back on it, I know she would of given me some. Damn! I was so dumb then.

(Pause) "And I tell you something else . . . don't be laughing, Harlan, cause if I hear you telling about me and . . . and what I ain't never had, your life ain't gon' be worth much. Cause the next day, I be putting your ass in the ground. And I will have all the gold! Ain't so funny now, is it?" Harlan wasn't surprised at Lefty's attitude. He knew Lefty had some interesting but disheartening experiences when he was younger, before they met. Lefty was a wild man, always losing his gold playing cards or drinking too much and, of course, waking up and discovering it was all gone. He says he sold the directions to a gold vein for what he thought was Union paper money. Turned out to be counterfeit. Harlan marveled at the way Lefty lived his life.

And by the time they got to Lisbon, they both realized the world was much larger than they had thought and much harder to get around in. It took them months! Of course, the boats they were on were old and much slower than they had realized, no matter the wind.

There was still the trip on land to the Portugal/Spanish border. How far that was? They had no idea, which didn't really bother them. They were accustomed to travelling without any appreciation for location or distance.

Lefty had thought often about returning to Rich Mountain getting the gold, all of it, and heading west and didn't understand why he couldn't bring himself to do that. He wasn't a really religious man but he knew, somehow, he knew, the good Lord wouldn't be happy with him if he were to abandon Harlan.

It was late evening when they disembarked in Lisbon and almost dark before that found transportation, which turned out to be a two wheeled buggy and a draft horse. And they decided to go as far as they could before sleeping. They traveled a couple of miles, maybe more; maybe less; they didn't really know. They weren't even sure if they were going in the right direction. They just kept going until they both fell asleep on the only seat the buggy had. When they woke up the next morning their horse was gone.

"I should have known better. You don't know nothing about keeping a two wheeled buggy and a horse safe." Lefty looked at Harlan with disgust. "So, what we do now?"

"I'm heading to the border. That's what we said we were going to do. Find me my perfect wife."

"Well, you do what you want. I'm gone get me some rest and then head back to Lisbon and catch the first thing that can carry me home. I'll leave your share of the gold in our secret place." Lefty stretched out on the seat, leaving no place for Harlan.

"You think I'm gone trust you with my gold? Here's what you and me gone do, Lefty. We gone do just as we planned, go find me the prettiest gal, that perfect one, in the world for me to marry. Then we go home. Got it?"

Lefty didn't respond. He moved around on the buggy's seat trying to find a comfortable place to sleep Blackie was on his way home from a little village on the Spanish/Portugal border where he had picked up a year-old working horse from one of his grandpa's customers. It was the first time he had entrusted him with such responsibility. In the past he had only stood around and did whatever his grandpa said. So, he was extra careful, wanting to prove he could be trusted to perform such responsibility. Consequently, he had to make sure he and the horse arrived safely. It wasn't an overnight trip, which would have been more challenging. He left home before daybreak with a big smile on his face. He was excited. When he got back with the horse in toll, it was still daylight. He wondered if his grandpa would start treating him like a man. Maybe they would have a drink of his grandpa's wine from his bottle. Maybe, but probably not!

His grandpa called him Blackie. Everybody did. And it didn't bother him. After all he did have dark skin, not black but real dark brown. He was the only dark person around anywhere, that he knew about. And that was the only name he knew to respond to. He may have had a different name but he doubted it. He was born in his grandpa shack. When? He didn't know.

His life seemed to start a few years ago when he started having strange accidents in bed. It would wake him up and he would be ashamed because it felt good but left a mess. And his grandpa would laugh at him and tell him to go wash his bedding. What he didn't understand was why his grandpa didn't get mad at him like before, when he was little. In those days he used to wet the bed all the time, probably every night. His grandpa didn't laugh at that. He would just beat the hell out of him, which didn't stop him from wetting in the bed. It was different, he knew that. One felt good and the other was just wet, messy.

His grandpa slapping him around for one accident and laughing at him for the other just seemed strange. Of course, there were lots of things that seemed strange about his grandpa, almost everything, like all the stories he would tell about his family. Not his daughter, Blackie's mother, he didn't have much to said about her! Once he did talk a little about her, just once.

According to his grandpa, she died four days or so after he, Blackie, was born. His grandpa always blamed her death on his birth, talking about his big feet trying to come out first. She had brought Blackie into the world anyway, feet first. And he had proven to be nothing but a damn curse that plagued his grandpa's life forever, at least, that's what his grandpa used to say. All the time he would say he, Blackie, was responsible for anything bad in his life.

"And look at me now. That's what you were going to say next. Right? I've heard that story, grandpa, all my life. It was the evening thing to do, your story-telling with a jug of wine on the table. Just for you!" On those days Blackie would have to do the cooking, which lately had become almost every day. His specialty was fried sardines and boiled potatoes with the skin still on and always covered with some kind of gravy or sauce or plain hot water and any kind of spice in it. He thought his grandpa would want him to use wine as the sauce one of these days. Never happened!

"But it's not a story, boy! You hear me? It's not a story, Goddamnit! It's the history, the history of one of the great families of Lisbon, Portugal. Used to be . . . I guess I should say that. And . . . if you wasn't so damn black and ugly that, being in this family, could have made you somebody, an important man. Me, too! But you're too damn black. Ask anybody in Lisbon, 'course they won't believe you're related to my family. They wouldn't even listen to that kind of talk. Wouldn't believe it. Look at yourself!!

"They know! They know the family. My family! Up in Lisbon, they know, even today they know. We just stopped here to bury my father. That was all. He was the leader, my father was. That's what we stopped here to do. Then we were going on to Spain or somewhere. Maybe to that new country, you know, where we could buy a piece of land and a slave or two, establish the family name over there. You know what? If I could get over there now, you could be my first slave! Hell, I don't even remember why we were going to Spain or wherever we were going. I don't know!

"What the hell were we going to do in Spain? Been thinking about that a long time. Spain, huh, don't remember. Anyway, I didn't want to be the one to let the family down. And I wasn't. It was your mama. That's who done it. My daughter! Your grandma, she must have turned over in her grave. A black in the family! We were a proud family back then. Look at us now!

"I was . . . am, I am from a family of wealth, so was my wife. Been so . . ."

"And you are just going through a few hard times, right? No matter you've been doing this for years." Blackie smiled at his grandpa and knew how happy talking made him or at least less grumpy.

"Well, I am. Me and my father and some other folks stopped here to let him rest some. He was sick; my father was. There were three wagons, I think."

"You told me you told them, including your wife, to keep going and you and your daddy would catch up later."

"She wasn't here, my wife wasn't. Don't know where she was." He looked at his glass that had been sitting in the same place for days. Only the bottle changed. "Listen you. Father, he was my father. I'm your granddaddy. See the difference?"

"I . . . don't think so. Don't really know."

Blackie's grandpa paused and looked at him as if he was trying to decide if he should explain. "He died that very day or was it the next day? I . . . anyway he died and that's when I started to drink."

"You said you started drinking earlier, when your grandfather didn't return from wherever he had gone. You also said it was when your wife left, you started."

"I told you all that? Guess I must have. How else would you know, unless your mother told you? But she didn't know, did she? Naw, she didn't know."

He sat in the chair. Blackie was standing behind him. He was shaking his head, as he picked up his wine bottle and dirty glass. "Your mother, she said she couldn't stand my drinking. Tired of it, she used to say. What the hell did she know?" He poured himself a glass full and drank it down without a pause, seemed like one huge gulp. "Hell, she was nothing like her mother. That's not true. She was as pretty as her. She was prettier, maybe. 'Course her mother, she never said a thing about my drinking. Married that woman down in Lisbon. A long time ago.

"She left too, not because she didn't like my drinking, she just didn't like me. My wife didn't, your grandmother. Don't know where she went. Some said she was headed for the coast to catch a boat somewhere. Other said she still in Lisbon. All I know is she left me. She's not here; that's all I know. Haven't seen her for years.

"Never missed her, Blackie. Not one day. But I miss your mama. I think about her, not always in a good way, but I do think about her. Never missed her mother. Never!

"A black fellow knocked on my door one morning with a note from her, my wife, your grandmother, asking me to send you to her. I told that black son of a bitch to be on his way or else. Didn't take him a minute to get back on his horse and get the hell out of here. You probably don't know this but a black man is supposed to be scared of a white man. That's why you scared of me. Didn't know that, did you? Never understood why! Anyway, that broken rail on the fence? The one you haven't fixed yet? Him and his horse did that."

"Grandpa, I thought you said she went with the others."

123

"Did I say that? When?" His grandpa looked puzzled.
"I'm frying up some sardines and potatoes. I'll wake you when they're ready."

"I don't need you to cook for me or tell me when to go to sleep or wake up. You just can't go around interrupting a man when he's talking, especially a white man. Your mama used to say I talked too much." He was laughing and pouring himself another glass of wine.

"Now, where was I? See that's why you can't just stop a man when he's talking.

"My . . . my grandfather was the captain of a ship, a freight ship, I think it was, running between Lisbon and the African Coast in search of African gold. Must have been easy to find 'cause he got rich. I don't know how many trips he made before he decided he wanted his own ship. Then the gold he found would be all his. But he didn't have enough to get the ship he wanted. He wanted the newest, the fastest."

Blackie noticed his grandpa entire demeanor had changed. He seemed somber and introspective and he even talked softer and slower. His eyes were focused on a spot or something on the floor in front of him. It was like he had forgotten Blackie was in the room.

"He went in with this Jew fellow, brought the fastest boat they could find. Then they headed for Africa, looking for gold. Never heard from them again. The family said he shouldn't of trusted that Jew. Don't know any Jews myself, never did.

"The good thing was that trip was supposed to be my father's maiden voyage but he got ill and couldn't go. That illness and my father's death plagued me until he died, right here in this village. Right out there on that road. I haven't been able to leave here since. Maybe you will, should. I hope you will." He looked up at Blackie and walked out of the door into the late evening with his wine bottle and glass in his hand.

Blackie never forgot that evening, and his grandpa never spoke of his family again, except for his daughter, Blackie's mama. Even after his grandpa died that was one of the things he would or could never forget.

Of course, from Blackie's perspective he didn't know what to think about all the stories his grandpa told him, the contradictions and what was importance and what wasn't. He did ask his grandpa about his own father once, just once, and he just looked at him, never said a word, just looked at him for a long while and then told him to find a mirror and look at it. Said that would tell him everything he needed to know about his daddy. But then he paused and smiled.

"Did I ever tell you about you mama, when she came back? Don't think I did. It was during Christmas time. I was walking home, just me and a bottle of wine. Christmas wine, made just for Christmas. Wasn't no different from the stuff I drank every day as far as I was concerned, 'cept it had a ribbon on it, a red one. But as I got closer, I could see smoke coming from my chimney. No smoke was supposed to be coming out of my chimney. Hell, I had to laugh out loud. 'Cause I knew it was her, your mama. I could have screamed for joy. So, I run to the door and open it. It was her alright with you in her belly, big as a house." I had to take a step backward. "Wasn't no joy after that. None! She wasn't supposed to have no baby! Not like you anyway! Then when you came out black as black could be with big feet, that was it. Damn, I was looking right at you when you came out, big feet first. Wasn't no mistake." That's all he would say about that. Never mentioned her again.

He never talked much about his father's father on his mother's side. Seemed like he didn't know what to say about him. He was the one, according to grandpa, that use to tell him a big blackbird dumped a heap of shit on my mother's head and it rained right after that washing the shit out of her hair, but leaving a seed that eased its way down between her legs and up inside her and grew into me. When his mother's father was on one of his mean drunks he would add that the seed went up the wrong hole and I came out looking like a black asshole. Then he would warn him to be on the lookout for a big blackbird that might come back looking for his son.

"But I tell you, 'course you know this, if I had a choice between you and my daughter, I'd choose her. Any day! Look at you, black son-of-a-bitch." His upper body would always shake from side to side and his eyes shot darts of hatred when he would call me that.

"And that's what she was, a bitch but a white one. I told her that. She would never listen to me. I was a drunkard to her. Claim she was scared of me. Hell, I wasn't gone do nothing to her, 'less she didn't do what I told her to do."

His grandpa did take care of him. That is, he lived in his grandpa's house that smelled like fertilizer, most of the time. More often than not, by bedtime his grandpa would be too drunk to take care of him.

For as long as he could remember, he had to work alongside of his grandpa, cleaning animal waste out of sheds and barns and yards and chicken coops. Actually, they did everything dirty that the villagers didn't want to do.

When Blackie got up some size his grandpa got a horse and wagon, how, he didn't know. Blackie's job was to fill that wagon up with animal waste. And once a week or so he would delivered it to farmers who used it as fertilizer, mixed in the soil which produced bigger and beautiful vegetables and fatter hogs.

But if it had not been for that young girl in the village, he would have been left alone to die, probably. She was the one that had tits full of milk and no one to give it to. Where she got all that milk nobody would say, not even her father who put her out of his house.

If there was a baby involved no one ever saw it or knew how she got it or where it went. Of course, there had to be one, but there was no evidence, except her tits full of milk. There were rumors. Always rumors!! She always played with the slave children. So, folks naturally assumed that had something to do with her not having a baby folk could see. And her daddy putting her out of his house and her being on her own at around twelve or thirteen led most folks to assume whatever they wanted. And that's when Blackie's grandpa came along. And it was sorta natural like, after all he did have Blackie.

She gladly gave her milk to Blackie, for a price. What that price was, no one knew. She told Blackie's grandpa she would give it to his little grandson whenever he needed it. Now that did cause a bit of a stir in the village. There were those who didn't like her sitting around with that little black baby grabbing her white tit. It was the same even if she was at grandpa's place, sitting out in the yard, white tit and little black baby. And that's where she was most of the time, at least, as long as Blackie could remember. His grandpa used to describe how little Blackie would grab hold to one of her red nipples and pull and suck away. Grandpa would then shake his head, look at Blackie and say something about it not looking right for a black baby to be sucking on a white tit, not in public. Of course, there were rumors about she and Blackie's grandpa. But there was no evidence of anything. And grandpa never admitted to anything. If he had, there was no doubt he would be hanging from a tree somewhere. The one thing that did happen was her tits got bigger and bigger. And on a young white girl that didn't look so good.

"I 'spect in some places you would of starved to death before they'd let you suck on a white tit. Other places they would of thrown your little black ass in the river or swamp. Somewhere, anywhere!"

Then when Blackie was sixteen or so, maybe older, he didn't know, he and the other boys in the village, who didn't care about his blackness yet, would have pissing contests. Who could pee the further. That's how he kind of figured out how old he was. But he could have been wrong because he could have been big or small for his age or have weak or strong peeing muscles. And he never won! Everybody else did, but not Blackie. Then the day he almost won was the day his grandpa sent for him to returned to the shack. He remembered it well because he had to quit during the final match. And if he had won that one he would have been champ for a day at least.

That was the day he had to go and finish his grandpa's work. Something had happened at the shack and Blackie decided his grandpa would want him to finish the work before coming home. Blackie did! How he knew what had not been done was a mystery. But he knew! Something told him it wasn't time for him to go back to the shack yet. By the time he got home from doing all that work, his grandpa was just sitting there in his chair with his head cocked to the side with that blank look in his eyes. His glass had rolled off the table and was on the floor, empty and dry. The wine jug was empty, too. Blackie had never seen that wine jug empty and his grandpa's glass on the floor, nor had he ever known his grandpa to be that quiet. He always had something to say when Blackie entered the shack. This time he said nothing, didn't even look in his direction. Blackie didn't know what to do.

"Want me to pick up your glass, Grandpa?" There was no answer and Blackie sensed a quiet stillness. Perhaps it was his grandpa's not talking, not moving. Perhaps not! Blackie proceeded to prepare his grandpa's meal.

"I'll leave your plate on the stove, Grandpa!" Still no answer "I'm going to take a walk, look around. You know, like we use to, me and you, walking together. except this time, it will be just me, walking by myself."

When he returned the shack was dark. He went immediately to bed, never looked around to see if anything had change.

And when his grandpa didn't wake him to go to work the next morning, and when he noticed his grandpa was in the same position, had on the same clothes, which weren't so unusual, the glass was still on the floor. Blackie eyes remained there, never looking up to see his Grandpa's face. Nothing had changed. And if nothing changed, everything must be alright.

Then after a few days there was a smell that he could barely stand but other people knew, just passing by the shack, they knew. They pointed at the shack and at him and kept their distance. The smell became overwhelming, his grandpa often had a foul odor but this was a different foul odor, he thought he had better have the young woman with the big breast look in on him, especially since when he peeked and discovered his grandpa had turned almost black. He knew his grandpa wouldn't want anybody seeing his all dark and all. And when she walked into the yard, she turned around immediately. She knew Blackie's grandpa was dead.

Blackie didn't know what to do and didn't want to spend his own little money for a village-style burial or any kind of burial. He had some men dig a hole and drop his grandpa in it. That was it. They put him in the ground that very day! Right out there on the other side of that broken fence. Where else could he go, smelling like he did, not to mention he had turned almost black, which made Blackie wonder if the big bird had paid his grandpa a visit.

Blackie was finally on his own in his grandpa's shack, which become his shack and most of the time, the lady who fed him when he was a baby and helped his grandpa around the shack and other things, didn't move in exactly, but she was always there. When he was a baby she had bathed him, but when he started to grow hair under his arms and other places, she would insist he bathe himself. She also insisted he bathe every Saturday in the kitchen during the winter and on the back porch in the summer, telling him nobody wanted to be around him smelling like his grandpa.

On occasions she would allow him to feel her tits and play with her pink nipples but just on occasions, especially when no one was around. It wasn't the same as it was when he was small. Her tits were not as firm and of course, the firmness of her body had turned into fat. But Blackie wanting to be near her had nothing to do with her changed body. It had everything to do with his just needing or wanting to be near her warm body, not any warm body but hers. He had grown up with that! Although his pant would protrude, sometimes, sticking out in front, she would slap his protrusion and push him away.

Blackie didn't seem to mind. All he wanted or needed was to be close to her, especially after his grandpa was gone. And she must have felt the same. They both seemed to enjoy his nestling his head in her bosom like he used to and touching her tit. She did tell him he was too old for that but they continued to get together often. Even though she knew he or she might want to do something else. She had seen him taking a bath and knew he was capable.

"You do know," she told him, "folk around here didn't like your mama bringing you here . . . just dumping you, leaving you. Some folk, lots of them, don't like my being here with you! But you have my milk running down and up your veins!" Then she would laugh really loud. He didn't know what to say. He did remember some of the things his grandpa used to say about his being black and her white tits. She had always been in his life.

He felt like he really needed to be close to someone, to have someone to hold him, which he never experienced from anyone but the woman with the tits. His grandpa had never touched him, never hugged him or kissed him on the cheek. Nothing! He used to say he never wanted him to. But that wasn't true. Sometime when his grandpa would get really drunk he would try and force him to put his arms around him, even then his grandpa resisted.

Blackie became a loner, with the exception of her, of course, spending his time trying to survive. He would hire himself out to those who could and would pay him to work for them and, of course, he still had what used to be his grandpa's work. So, he was always busy!

One of the opportunities often offered to Blackie's grandpa required him to take a horse and wagon and pick up packages and dry goods from a merchant who had a place on the outskirts of Lisbon. He remembered his grandpa responding positively only once, declaring the trip took too many days and brought back too many memories. He refused so many times that villagers stopped asking him. But after his grandpa died, they asked Blackie to consider it and offered him more money. His answer was an immediate and resounding "Yes!", not because of the money but the opportunity to take a trip, to see things he had never seen before, meet different people and maybe look into the family his grandpa talked about. But that was the most terrifying, checking on his family as his grandpa had described them. Of course, he knew they wouldn't recognize him. After all, he was black.

On the morning of his first trip, the woman with the tits declared she was going with him.

"No, you can't go with me." Blackie was emphatic in his response.

"You don't even know how to get there. Do you?" She knew he didn't because she had been with him all of his life. And he had never been to Lisbon or anywhere in that direction. Neither had she.

"My grandpa told me that road right out there goes straight to the road to Lisbon. He said that's how he got here, to this very spot. So, I'll be okay."

"Then what?" She looked at him with an air of confidence.

"What you mean, then what?" Blackie was concerned.

"I know you don't know anything about out there." She sniggered and looked away.

"You don't know that. I can find out things. Grandpa told me things!"

"Yeah, I know what he told you. Some of it, at least. But I already know the way."

"Good for you?"

"Due west. About three miles. Then the road to Lisbon."

"How do you know that?"

"I know lots of things you don't know. I'm older than you."

"So?"

"And I want to know more. That's why I want to leave here. Live in a big city. Meet different people. Have a different life." She was jubilant, smiling and moving around, excited.

"And you wouldn't be coming back?"

"Nope!"

"Okay, okay, but . . . I don't know."

"You don't have to know. I do! I've always known more than you!"

Blackie relented. She was extremely happy, but he was apprehensive.

They travelled all day and into the evening hours. She had been so confident that he would say yes, she had prepared a big basket of food and had blankets to keep them warm at night. He had thought of none of that and their importance became obvious the first night. They slept on the wagon bed with his hand on her breast and covered with her blankets, as always.

The road to Lisbon was easy to find. There was a sign that said Lisbon and an arrow indicating the direction. Of course, Blackie couldn't read but his grandpa had said something about that sign and what it said. She could read some. She had been in school before her father sent her away from his house. She knew what the sign said. She had smiled at Blackie.

About a mile or so down that road, Blackie saw a horseless buggy and stopped. She encouraged him to keep going.

"Nobody meaning anything good would leave a buggy like that on the road. Don't feel right. I say keep going."

"You don't tell me what to do. You just like grandpa. Always telling me something. I don't have to listen anymore, not to him or you." He handed her the reins and climbed down off the wagon and walked over to the horseless buggy.

"What you looking for? Ain't nothing there. You better come on before I leave you."

"You better not leave me."

"Well, I will." She started the horse forward slowly, hoping Blackie would return. He didn't. She gave the horse one quick slap with the whip and she was gone.

Blackie stood there speechless for a moment, then laughed and returned to inspecting the buggy, assuming she would return. She didn't.

Blackie ran to the middle of the road and all he could see was a cloud of dust.

"Did you think she was really coming back? You can't trust a woman like that." It took Lefty a moment or two, standing behind him, to realize he was black.

"Why not? You know her?" Blackie's body became tense, but he didn't turn around, not right away.

"I told you we needed to get a jump on them. All we got now is this nigger." Harlan shook his head.

"What?" Then Blackie turned around to face them. "What's a nigger? I never heard that before."

"You don't know . . . back where I'm from, it's a person who looks like you."

"Oh, I see! Because I'm black. My grandpa never said anything about that. Where you from?"

"Hush, Harlan, we could have used that damn horse, maybe the wagon too." Walking up to Blackie who seemed to ignore both of them and returned his focus on looking down the road.

"You live close by? What you doing out here with a white woman?"

Blackie continued to ignore them. He was waiting, sort of looking down the road for her but listening to them talk. He thought, he was pretty sure she would be back after she had her little fun.

"This nigger here must be deaf or something." Harlan looked at Lefty for confirmation.

"Don't call him that. He don't even look like them. Look at his hair and nose. I don't think they got niggers over here, not like we got. Hell, he don't have lips, not big ones!" Lefty looked at Harlan with some disgust.

"Where's your horse? You best find him and move on." Blackie spoke with confidence but didn't look at them. He just continued his walked down the road. It was like they had just been dismissed.

"Hey, boy. Stop right there! Damnit! It ain't none of your business where our horse is. You best be worried about your horse and wagon . . . and us. Where I'm from . . ."

"Hush, Harlan, let me do all the talking. You live nearby? Where was yawl going? You and that white woman!"

"Lisbon! That's where we started to. Suppose to pick up some stuff for some forks in the village." Blackie continued to walk down the road. The wagon's dust had disappeared a long time ago. All he could do was hope she would be waiting for him on some side road, laughing.

"We just left there a couple of days ago. Somebody stole our horse while we slept. Any thought about who might of done that? Help us out here and we might give you a piece of gold. Got plenty of that." He smiled at Blackie who kept walking.

"We better be on the lookout." Harlan still walked behind them. "No telling what he got planned. Betcha there's a whole bunch of them hiding somewhere." He stopped. "We might be walking into a trap or something. Can't trust no nigger. Don't care where they at."

Lefty stopped, too.

Blackie kept walking. It was like they weren't there. Harlan pulls out his pistol and aimed it at Blackie's back but Lefty stopped him. "Mister . . ."

"I'm not a mister yet. I don't think. My grandpa never told me when I would become a mister. She didn't either. I thought she would have when the time was right but she never did. Guess she forgot about it or the time wasn't right yet. Now she's gone. Guess I'll never get to be a mister, huh?" Blackie stopped walking but still didn't turn around.

"Her? Who?" Lefty pointed up the road. "The woman who took your wagon? Look, what's your name?" Lefty put on his best kind and friendly demeanor.

"We been waiting for someone to show up. We even prayed for the good Lord to send us somebody. And lo and behold here you are. The good Lord sent you to help us find that horse and anything else we need. Just like back home. This ain't the first time He sent nig . . . folk like you to help us whites. What would we do without yawl? That's the way God made the world. You help us build his kingdom. And he blesses all of us . . . in his way."

"I don't know nothing about being sent to help anybody. Grandpa never said nothing about helping others. He never said anything about this . . . God person either."

"Told you, damnit. I don't know what the good Lord got to do with this. So now we have to figure out how to get to my perfect wife." Harlan interjected.

"Unless in His wisdom . . . he's telling us He don't want us to go to Spain." Lefty spoke calmly to Harlan but loud enough for Blackie to hear. "So please, let me work with our Lord and Savior. You know I'm a Christian man, Harlan. Always was!"

Blackie heard all of this. They were talking to each other like he wasn't even there.

"I don't know nothing about this God you talking about. Never met Him myself. What is it you all want? I don't have anything."

"How close is your place. You got animals, food, horses, you know?"

"Ain't got nothing but a shack. Use to belong to my grandpa. He's dead." When Blackie stopped he suddenly realized they were all in the same situation. No horse! Plus, the thought did cross his mind that they may be his only way of finding some other place to go, away from her and his grandpa. Maybe he won't have to go back either. But Spain? He didn't want to go to Spain. Been there!

"If you can tell us where we can find a horse and a wagon, there may be something in it for you. Gold! You know what that is, right?"

"Grandpa, he was from a family that had gold, 'til his grandpa brought a ship. He and a Jewish man went in together."

"A ship? A Jew? That don't sound good. What for?"

"They went to Africa looking for gold. Never came back."

"Africa? That's where our slaves come from. Now that's God's gold!"

"Then grandpa fell on hard times. He had to work every day. All day! And everything, all of it, went in the wine bottle. But besides him, his folks had money. They knew about gold."

"Oh, so you going to Lisbon to be with those folks? And the woman who took the horse and the wagon?"

"Just a lady from the village. She . . . She helped me and my grandpa some times."

"What the hell's wrong with you, Lefty? We ain't got no time to be hanging around here and listening to this stuff."

"Ain't nothing wrong with me, Harlan. You know how I am, always thinking ahead. Do you think this here boy's strange, you know, different? 'Cause I ain't never seen no black people with straight hair and I've been all over back home. I know there's some half whites, probably left a few myself. But not like this one."

"Don't you start with that crazy thinking, Lefty. The last time you got to thinking about stuff almost got us put in jail and we could of lost all our gold."

"Yeah, well, you right. But where you think he came from? If it wasn't for his straight black hair and little nose, and them funny colored eyes, and look at them thin lips, he'd look just like those nigger slaves and we know what they look like back home. Right?"

"Yeah, but his hair is as straight as mine. I don't know what you're thinking; but just leave it be, Lefty. Sometimes I don't think you ought to think so much."

"Ain't no blacks around these parts that I know of. They're all down by the docks and ships. Ain't got no straight hair either. But he does! So, where he come from? 'Course I ain't never been in these parts before but I got a feeling."

"That's worse than you thinking a lot. You ain't never done anything right on your feeling." Harlan didn't appear to be comfortable.

"Hush, Harlan, can't you see I'm thinking?"
"And feeling. That's what I'm worry about."
"They got hard, tight nappy hair, right? Back home, I mean!"

Lefty spoke with certainty. "Yeah! How you know that? Could be just look like that. You been rubbing nigger heads or something? You did, didn't you? Just to see."

"Lookit! He ain't like them. He ain't! See? And the other thing is he sounds different too. You know the way he talks. They say, and I don't know this for a fact, but they do say that nappy hair pulls on the brain. Locks the brains up, you know, so it don't work right. Made sense to me. Us? Straight hair, brain free to work! I don't remember where I heard that." He ran his hand through his dirty brown hair, pulling it down and out so he could see it."

"I don't know about that. This nigger here, he ain't never been beaten. I think the son of a bitch is crazy. He's standing there in the middle of the road listening to everything we say and ain't said nothing. Like he don't know nothing! He knows! Betcha if I beat his ass he'll know! Where that boy from? He worried about that woman and that horse. He better be worrying about me putting my boot in his ass!" Harlan stopped talking. Looked at Lefty. "Anyway, he ain't got nothing to do with why we came over here. We're going where the pretty ladies is! Got it, Lefty" He turned away in disgust.

"I know, I know!"

"Lefty, I tell you, and I ain't playing, if the women in Spain ain't as pretty as you say, you gonna be in real trouble."

"Hold on there, Harlan, I ain't said nothing about them having pretty women. Don't put that on me."

Harlan kept talking. It was as if Lefty hadn't said a word.

"I didn't come all this way for nothing! I got enough gold to get anything I want, wherever I want! I'm looking for something special. And you said, Lefty, that Spain was that special place. And remember, Lefty, I'll leave your ass over here and nobody will be able to find you." He looked at Lefty with direct no-nonsense eyes.

Of course, he was bigger than Lefty and looked more menacing. He had big arms and a barrel chest and thick neck! Lefty was a little fellow, looking like he had never eaten a good meal, just kind of skin and bone. He used to carry a pistol but lost it in a card game. So, he took up with Harlan for protection until he could get his gun back. But they found that gold. And Lefty never thought about his gun again. He had Harlan and gold.

"Don't worry you'll have plenty to pick from!" Lefty spoke with confidence.

"How do you know that? You said you never been there."

"Trust me, Harlan. After all this time, you know I will bring us through. I've talked to Spaniards all over the world and they all told me how pretty their women are. I know!"

"Why we standing around here? We could of walked to Spain by now." Harlan's impatience was obvious.

"That's where we was headed, 'til someone took our horse." Lefty looked at Blackie.

"Spain. Grandpa said some of his people might have gone there. He didn't really know. Maybe."

Blackie started walking toward Lisbon again.

He needed to find the woman with the tit, his wagon and horse. That's what he felt he should do, what his heart told him to do. Then he could go back to the life he lived in his grandpa's shack or stay in Lisbon or do whatever he wanted. The thought of doing whatever he wanted excited him but also frightened him. What would he do? His grandpa never talked about anything like that.

He wouldn't be leaving anything behind. He didn't have anything to leave. But his grandpa's spirit! And the woman who gave him tit? He knew she wasn't coming back. She took the horse by the rein and simply left.

"What about the woman in the wagon? She coming back?" Lefty was hopeful.

"What for? What we need to do is get on our way to Spain. I ain't gon' keep telling you that, Lefty." Harlan seemed even more impatience and serious.

Holding his hand out in a stopping matter. "Wait a minute! Just hold on. Maybe . . . what I am thinking, and I need your help with this, Harlan, 'cause you're a pretty good straight shooter."

"Don't be trying to make me feel important."

"Just listen. What if we took him with us to Spain? Huh? After we get your woman . . . "

"She ain't just some old woman, Lefty! She'll be the prettiest woman in the world! Perfect!"

"I know, I know!"

"Well, you best start acting like it. I'm getting tired of this."

"Just listen to me. It'll all come together. Listen, just listen! We take him to Spain with us. Then, we all head for home with them both in tow. We can sell or loan him out as a breeder. Ain't many blacks people with straight hair, them funny looking eyes and talk the way he do. Can't beat that, huh? And . . . and he got straight hair! Just think of the breeding he can do and have fun doing it and we get richer, especially if they believe that straight hair is the thing that makes the brain work. See what I mean?" Lefty was clearly excited about the prospects.

It was a moment or two before Harlan responded, shaking his head, almost in sympathy. "Them slave owners, they don't want nothing to do with smart niggers. They want em' dumb. The dumber the better."

"Well, yeah but . . . " Lefty interrupted him.

"Ain't no butts, Lefty. It is what it is. You listen to me. If we go the way they came we bound to find something. This nigger and that woman, they came from somewhere. You hear me?"

Sensing Harlan's concern, Lefty took several steps toward him and placed his right hand of assurance on Harlan's shoulder. He could feel Harlan relaxing.

"Think about it, Harlan."

"Think about what? I done made up my mind."

"You know. The first thing we planned to do with that gold was buy some land and get some niggers to slave for us. The only thing missing, you said, was a wife. Remember?"

"Course, I remember, and you said the best, most beautiful girls was in Spain. And we're on our way, almost there."

"Never in life did I think it would take all this to find you a wife. Hey, you, wait a minute! Where you think you going?" Blackie had put some distance between them. Lefty looked at Harlan and down the road at Blackie's back.

"We can't just let him walk off like that. He could lead us to some horses."

"Not going that way. And we know about horses in Lisbon." Harlan seemed a bit more relaxed. "Rich men like us, we sometime waste gold on things we know ain't right. That's what rich men like us do. I know! What you think, I don't have no sense? I know what I'm doing."

Blackie stopped and turned around, waiting on their next move. He had been thinking about not going back to the village, just keep walking toward Lisbon.

There was nothing in the village for him, not even a mate, nothing but memories of his grandpa and the stuff he had to deal with to make a living. Everyone in the village expected him to follow in his grandpa's footsteps. And no one in the village would ever call him Mister.

He had chuckled to himself when he thought about going on his own. Where would he go? Lisbon was the only possibility, unless he went with the strangers. He would be on his own, except they would determine what that meant, much like his grandpa did.

"Well, Harlan and me, we been thinking and talking about going on to Spain. Hell, if all he wants is a good looking woman, well, he can find one of them anywhere, except around here, it seems, especially if the woman who took the horse is an example."

"She got them sagging tits now and a little heavy on the back side." Harlan laughed.

"Yeah, but . . . " Lefty wasn't sure what to say but he knew she was better than nothing.

"Ain't no buts! I know! She said I was the cause. Grandpa said my mother died when I was really young and that woman, the one that took the wagon, gave me tit when I was a baby. She . . . she let me touch her tit, after I got up some size, too."

"And?" Lefty's interest perked up.

"And what?"

"What happened after you did that? You know, felt her tits." Lefty was getting excited.

"Ain't nothing happened. What was supposed to?"

"Lord, have mercy, you don't know, do you? Huh, huh, huh! Tell you what we gonna do. When she comes this evening, we'll all grab her. See? I'll do it first, then you, and then Harlan; 'cept Harlan will probably want to go after me and then you can do it last. How about that?"

"How about what? Do what? She's not coming back." He wasn't that innocent, he knew exactly what Lefty was talking about and didn't like it.

"I'll have the wagon and everything ready to go. We tie her up, gag her, put you and her in the back and when we get way down the road, before daybreak, let her out and we go on down the road to the docks, catch a ship to England. By the time she gets back to the village and tells somebody, we be out to sea somewhere. See?"

"She ain't coming back."

"Don't worry about him. We've done this before, many times. If you pick the right woman, ain't nobody caring. She won't care."

Blackie looked at him and at Harlan who was still standing where Lefty left him. Blackie shook his head sympathetically and started a slow run toward Lisbon. He had no idea how far that was and knew he would soon run out of energy. But he needed to put some distance between them.

Lefty was alone! Harlan had turned and started walking in the opposite direction toward Spain. Lefty seemed to be talking to himself, certainly not loud enough for neither Blackie or Harlan to hear.

"Naw, we will probably be doing her a favor. Back home, if a white woman gives tit to a nigger, she'll be doomed. Hold it there! Your hair is straight. Over there the blacks got nappy hair. That's why they so dumb. It's the way their hair pulls on their brain. You hear me?" He knew no one did.

The evening came but soon disappeared into a beautiful star filled night. Blackie had stopped to relieve himself and rest. And when he looked down the road for Lefty and Harlan, they were nowhere to be seen. He found a place where he could sit against a tree and relax. But before long he was fast asleep.

"And you better protect me." She was looking down directly at Blackie. "Come on, we better get going." She moved quickly to the road looking as if she expected to see Lefty and Harlan.

"No one's coming for us, if that's what you're worried about?" Blackie was certain that Lefty and Harlan had decided to get to Spain as fast as they could, find Harlan a wife, get some horses and head back to the Lisbon coast for their trip home. He had no way of knowing that but concluded it was a good thought, the right thought, and maybe the only one.

She sat down next to him. "You thought I was gone, huh? Well, I was. But then I decided I didn't want you to be like your grandpa, not with my milk running through your vein. So . . . here I am."

She seemed relaxed, having said something that always weighted on her heart. She had given her milk to him. They had a connection. And, clearly, they were glad to see each other.

"What are we going to do now? We just can't stay here. And I got places I want to go, like I told you." She looked firmly at Blackie.

"Where? Where you want to go?" Blackie suddenly realized he had no place to go, unless he went with her.

"I don't know. I've never been far from the village but I think it'll be okay, seeing new things and now that you are a man . . . " She stood there as he walked passed her into the early evening sun.

When Blackie got to the road, all he could see were the shadows of trees stretching softly across its width. The empty road and the tree shadows, some long, some short hypnotized him for a moment with its calmness and beauty and stillness. He wanted to act like he wasn't afraid and nervous, wondering if Lefty and Harlan would come after them and if he would be able to manage without his grandpa's shack to shield him. He wanted to stand and not show fear. But it was there. Deep inside him. And It would always be there.

"Well, let's rest a bit and get started down the road in the norming." He turned away from her, hoping she would not see the fear on his face. Sometimes during the night, she had gotten the blankets and covered them.

The quietness of the night give way to the pleasant night sounds. He had heard those sounds before at his grandpa's shack but they were unwelcomed, often intrusive and, consequently, more disturbing than not. But under the brightness and beauty of the night, the sounds were like new, nothing like he had heard at his grandpa's shack, his home.

The warmth of the sun woke them the next morning and there was a distinct and pleasant difference, not at all like waking up in the shack. He liked the sound. Its beauty would not be ignored. Their first move was to walk to the road and look for Lefty and Harlan. But the road was clear, except for the low clouds of dust stirred up by a slight wind.

Even with the slight wind and increasing warmth from the sun, it was a quiet leisurely ride that day. The wagon moved with ease, its springs and wheels making a sound that became an expected musical background along with the feel of the wagon as it rolled over pot holes, small tree branches and other debris in the road.

"I guess this road would be hard to travel after a good rain. I don't see one coming this way. Sky's really blue." Blackie spoke with confidence. "Guess we don't have to worried about that, huh? The rain, I mean"

"What does rain look like when it's coming at you? Never thought about that before. The shack just had leaks here and there, dripping sounds, sometimes like sad music. " She didn't look at him when she spoke. She just shook her head and looked away.

"You and grandpa thought I didn't know anything, huh? Guess I thought the same thing. But looking back on it. I don't know. That's a whole lot of ways to learn stuff, even from what he used to say."

"And he would say things to you I would overhear and wonder about. Sometimes I wondered how you survived. Won't hear those things in Lisbon.

"Maybe not. Except if I try to contact grandpa's family, at least the one he used to talk to me about. Don't need to anyway! I got that connection with you."

By late evening they started to see other wagons and men on horses. And in the distance, there were lights flickering against a darkling sky.

"That must be Lisbon." Blackie stopped in the middle of the road and looked in the distance, then turned and looked behind him. "Came a longways today, huh?"

"Must be what?" She thought she should be happy with joy pumping and increasing her heart beat forcing a grin to stretch across her face. But she couldn't even manage a smile. She had never seen anything like what was before her, the lights, the people moving around, going places, doing things.

"I don't know." He sensed her apprehension and wondered if she sensed his. They sat there for a moment or two looking at the flickering lights against a darkening sky. "Feels different, don't it?"

Then Blackie made that special clicking sound that urged the horse forward, headed for the flickering lights.

(It's been a long time coming, but a change is coming! I know…)

CPSIA information can be obtained
at www.ICGtesting.com
Printed in the USA
BVHW082319310521
608489BV00014B/2261